Four Seasons of Ministry

Four Seasons of Ministry

Gathering a Harvest of Righteousness

BRUCE G. EPPERLY

and

KATHERINE GOULD EPPERLY

THE
ALBAN
INSTITUTE
Herndon, Virginia
www.alban.org

The Alban Institute
2121 Cooperative Way, Suite 100
Herndon, VA 20171

Scripture quotations, unless otherwise noted, are from the New Revised Standard Version of the Bible, copyright © 1989, Division of Christian Education of the National Council of Churches of Christ in the United States of America, and are used by permission.

Cover design by Spark Design, LLC.

5-23-12

Library of Congress Cataloging-in-Publication Data

Epperly, Bruce Gordon.
    Four seasons of ministry : gathering a harvest of righteousness / Bruce
G. Epperly and Katherine Gould Epperly.
        p. cm.
    Includes bibliographical references.
    ISBN 978-1-56699-366-1
    1. Pastoral theology. I. Epperly, Katherine Gould, 1950- II. Title.

BV4011.3.E65 2008
253'.2--dc22
                                        2008023664

12   11   10   09   08   VP   1   2   3   4   5

Contents

A Word of Invitation
and Thanks

To everything, there is a season! As we complete this book, the church has recently observed the Feast of Epiphany and celebrated its affirmation that insight and revelation are global and yet intimate in nature. Like the magi, the two of us—and countless other pastors—have come from afar, following the star of vocation, and have taken many unexpected routes in our quest to be faithful not only to God but also to our families and to our calling to be spiritual leaders in this dynamic, pluralistic, and uncertain time.

In this text the two of us reflect on the spiritual and vocational adventures of pastors as they journey through the four seasons of ministry—first the call to ordained ministry and seminary preparation, then the transition from seminary to first congregational call, then midcareer flourishing in ministry, and finally preparation for retirement and beyond. To prepare for writing this text, we interviewed and met with more than one hundred pastors in every season of ministry. Our narratives describe their quest to be faithful pastors committed not only to excellence in the arts and practices of ministry but also to personal and relational well-being and to spiritual growth. Our hope is that in hearing their stories you will be inspired to seek spiritual wholeness and professional and personal vitality and excellence in your current season as a pastor.

We believe that God is present in every season of ministry and that faithful and healthy ministry is the result of the lively and dynamic interplay of call and response—and grace and intentionality—that characterize the quest for excellence, well-being, and effectiveness in ministry. Accordingly, this text weaves together theological reflection, spiritual formation, ministerial practices, and the concrete experiences of faithful pastors.

Every author has her or his perspective that shapes, explicitly or implicitly, her or his vision of theology, spirituality, and ministry. Our approach to nurturing faithful spirit-centered ministry arises out of nearly sixty years of combined ministerial experience in academic, congregational, and seminary settings. Ordained in 1980, Bruce is a theologian and spiritual guide who has integrated teaching and administration with hands-on congregational, university, and interim ministry. His theology of healing and wholeness shapes his ministry, and his congregational ministry concretizes his theology. Bruce currently directs and leads programs aimed at ministerial excellence and spiritual formation for newly ordained ministers, pastors in midcareer, and pastors preparing for retirement through Lancaster Theological Seminary's Office of Continuing Education. Ordained in 1979, Kate is a congregational pastor, spiritual director, and pastoral counselor trained in a variety of complementary health modalities that integrate body, mind, and spirit. Kate assists Bruce in leading three ministerial excellence groups for new pastors within the Lancaster Seminary program. Both of us are reiki healing touch master-teachers whose commitment to healing and wholeness has shaped our approach to nurturing the practice of ministerial excellence, transformation, and well-being.[1]

Our understanding of ministry has been influenced by process-relational theology, congregational and family systems theory, Jungian psychology, the developmental spirituality of James Fowler, Carol Gilligan, and Erik Erikson, and the healing ministry of Jesus. We count John Cobb, Howard Thurman, Isabella Bates, and Gerald May among our mentors.

The development and writing of this book reflects our experiences, approaches, and partnership in life and ministry. Bruce was the primary visionary, architect, and builder of the text, while Kate provided interior design and creative adornment as well as substantive narrative content, making this house of words a spiritual home.

Many insights came on Bruce's early morning contemplative walks and our daily couple's sharing and planning walks that have, over the years, become a vital part of our marital and professional partnership. The book as a whole, and each page, reflects our different yet complementary personalities, gifts, and work styles as well as our commitment to God's vision for healthy pastors and healthy congregations.

In the course of this book as we describe the journeys of pastors throughout the four seasons of ordained ministry, we have told our own stories and related the stories of certain named pastors, including Gordon, Monica, and Megan. However, for the most of pastors whose stories we tell, we have altered their names, locations, and gender, and occasionally their denominational affiliations, so that their privacy is ensured. In a few cases, our narrative describes composites of several pastors who share common experiences and challenges despite their differences in denomination, age, gender, and geographical location.

As we finish this book on the Feast of Epiphany, we are reminded of how the profoundly dynamic and shifting energy of life shapes our vocation as pastors. Our only son, Matthew, is on the verge of finishing the last of four cycles of chemotherapy for germ cell cancer. As we began writing this book in early 2007, we were looking forward to celebrating his wedding with Ingrid in July 2007. We now conclude this text in January 2008 with great hope for a cure. When we began this text, we could never have imagined the challenges of the past three months during which we have had to balance writing responsibilities, teaching and administration, and marriage and ministry with care and support for Matthew and Ingrid. This book is an all-too-fresh witness to the many unanticipated challenges pastors face in their quest to join faithful ministry with care for children, spouses, and themselves. During the past three months, we have experienced the generosity of friends and colleagues. Our congregation, Disciples United Community Church, Lancaster, Pennsylvania, and Lancaster Theological Seminary have embodied the grace and understanding that enabled us to do good work as pastors and academics, to finish this book, and to be faithful to our family in a time of crisis. The institutions in which we minister embody Christian *koinonia* and compassion at their best.

This book is the result of not only our unique partnership and synergy as a clergy couple but also our many creative and trusting relationships with pastors in Lancaster Theological Seminary's ministerial excellence groups, which are supported through the generous commitment of the Lilly Endowment, under the direction and guidance of Craig Dykstra and John Wimmer. The participants in these ministerial groups designed to support clergy in every season of ministry have inspired, challenged, and taught us many things about ministerial fidelity and excellence over the past four years.

We have been blessed to share many honest and supportive conversations with pastors across the United States and Canada over the past thirty years. We have been guided and inspired by their wisdom and commitment to ministry. In contrast to commentators who bemoan the current state of ministry, we have found today's pastors in every season of ministry to be persons of faith, maturity, and dedication. Their giftedness and commitment give us hope for the future of the church.

Bruce is particularly grateful to his colleagues at Lancaster Theological Seminary and is most especially thankful for the support and leadership of President Riess Potterveld and Academic Dean Edwin David Aponte.[2] The two of us appreciate the work of Rollin Russell in initiating the program Bruce now directs as well as the commitment of Peter Schmiechen and David Rich in helping plan and lead creative programs for pastors considering retirement. Bruce is grateful for the personal and professional support of his Continuing Education colleagues, David Mellott and Rikki Jones.

We are both deeply thankful to Richard Bass, director of publishing at the Alban Institute, for his encouragement, support, and creativity at every stage of this book and to Andrea Lee's careful and insightful editing of the manuscript.

We recognize too the gift of theological and spiritual freedom given us by our congregation, Disciples United Community Church, a progressive, open, and affirming United Church of Christ and Disciples of Christ congregation in Lancaster. This open-spirited community has encouraged us to express ourselves theologically and spiritually without apology and has enabled us to be our best in the practice of ministry.[3]

Recognizing the wider web of life that has brought us to this place and time, we also thank our parents, living and deceased. Bruce is especially grateful for the encouragement he received from his Baptist minister father, Everett Epperly, and the prayers of his mother, Loretta Baxter Epperly, that still live on in his teaching, administration, and ministry. Bruce and Kate are grateful for the endless supply of emotional and spiritual support given by Kate's ninety-year-old mother, Maxine, who lives with us. We are blessed by the love that has emerged in our growing relationship with our son, Matt, and the growing circle of love embodied in his marriage to Ingrid.

We conclude our thanksgiving with a prayer for our readers: May you experience God's inspiration and companionship in every season of life so that you can run the race of spiritual leadership, whether as a pastor, spouse or partner, family member, or layperson, with excellence, grace, energy, inspiration, and love.

Feast of Epiphany 2008
Lancaster, Pennsylvania

⫷ 1 ⫸

The Four Seasons of Ministry

I am confident of this, that the one who began a good work among you will bring it to completion by the day of Jesus Christ. . . . And this is my prayer, that your love may overflow more and more with knowledge and full insight to help you determine what is best, so that in the day of Christ you may be pure and blameless, having produced the harvest of righteousness that comes through Jesus Christ for the glory and praise of God.

—Philippians 1:6, 9-11

On a cold February day, during the last good snow of the wintry season, Gordon Forbes gazed in the distance as he looked back on nearly fifty years of ordained ministry. As we shared soup and salad at a Bethesda, Maryland, bistro, Gordon shared his vision of ministry—past, present, and future. We chose Gordon, a European-American United Church of Christ pastor, for our first interview because he exemplified ministry at its best over an entire career. Gordon clearly had lived creatively through the seasons of ordained ministry from the time of his original experience of call to concluding his full-time professional career and having deep confidence that he had been faithful to his calling and could look back on a well-lived pastoral adventure.

The two of us knew firsthand about Gordon's integrity and skill in ministry because he had been our pastor at Westmoreland United Church of Christ during Bruce's seventeen years as Protestant university chaplain at Georgetown University and Kate's many years as a congregational minister and pastoral counselor in the Washington, D.C., suburbs. Jan, his wife of nearly fifty years, had been our son Matt's preschool music teacher. Over his seventeen years as pastor at Westmoreland, we had witnessed Gordon as an insightful preacher, a poet, a forceful advocate of social justice, and a firm, yet fair and supportive, administrator and senior pastor of a large, multistaff congregation. Gordon had ministered to Washington, D.C., powerbrokers and homeless persons alike, and he had provided guidance and pastoral care to our family in times of transition and crisis. Gordon had practiced the art of ministry with grace and integrity. Now, Gordon was embracing the winter of ministry with the same joy and vitality that he once welcomed his ministry's spring.

Gordon is a large man with a big personality, but more than that, he is a person of spiritual stature, with a soul large enough to pastor a challenging and complex congregation, to work for social justice, to practice regular spiritual disciplines, to mentor young pastors, and to provide national and local denominational leadership. We trusted Gordon as a pastor, friend, church leader, and spiritual elder who talked the talk and walked the walk of progressive, socially concerned, and spiritually centered Christianity.

At age seventy-three, Gordon is still looking toward the future. Since his retirement as senior pastor of Westmoreland United Church of Christ in 1999, Gordon and Jan have begun each day prayerfully reading Scripture in the spirit of *lectio divina*, a traditional practice of spiritual reflection, based on the Rule of St. Benedict.[1] The practice of *lectio divina* involves reading Scripture meditatively and listening for God's personal word to us in our particular time and place. Gordon and Jan are still listening for the "sighs too deep for words" that will guide them on the next steps of their spiritual adventure (Rom. 8:26).

Biblical scholar and theologian Marcus Borg describes Jesus as a "spirit person" whose transparency to God enabled others to experience God's presence in their own lives. Gordon Forbes is also a "spirit person" who in 1972, during a time of spiritual and vocational dislocation, discovered the importance of spiritual practices as essential to ministerial excellence. Two pivotal events transformed his way of looking at life and ministry. Both encounters related to the interplay of political involvement and pastoral ministry. As chair of the Minnesota Democratic-Farmer-Labor Party, Gordon had led the fight for equal rights for gay and lesbian persons, a fight that had been hard and costly for Gordon, both personally and professionally. Further, in the wake of Richard Nixon's landslide victory over George McGovern in the U.S. presidential election, Gordon, then in his late thirties with a dozen years of ministry behind him, was feeling depleted, depressed, and uncertain where to go in his life and ministry. In the midst of his personal and professional "dark night of the soul," Gordon discovered the psalms of lament as a resource for prayer. True to theologian and social activist Robert McAfee Brown's insight that the "surprises of grace" often emerge when a person feels most spiritually dislocated, Gordon discovered God's grace anew through praying the psalms of loss and disorientation. By prayerfully reading the psalms, he found that he could place the totality of his emotional life before God, whether he felt anger or elation, despair or victory, loneliness or companionship.

About the same time, a woman who had been faithfully attending his congregation in Northfield, Minnesota, asked him about qualifications for membership in the congregation. Gordon was shocked when she queried, "Do I have to be a Democrat to join this church?" Gordon recalls that he decided then and there to reaffirm his call to "first, be a pastor!" Through all his adventures of ministry, Gordon has stuck by that unexpected insight: "First, be a pastor," regardless of personal, civic, or political involvements. Today, "first, be a pastor" is still Gordon's one piece of advice to newly ordained ministers. "Let the people know you want to be involved in their lives. Maintain your integrity, but always be compassionate and direct even to those who oppose you," Gordon counsels.

The Forbes and Epperly families both moved to Washington, D.C., in 1982. Gordon notes that his commitment to social justice initially tempted him to become overly involved in the national and local political scene. Knowing how seductive politics could be for his pastoral ministry, Gordon followed the guidance of a colleague who suggested that he become involved in the spiritual growth programs at the Shalem Institute for Spiritual Formation.[2] Although Gordon has never backed away from political involvement and taking difficult social and political stands, he also affirms that his spiritual practices sustained him during his seventeen years as pastor of a highly educated, demanding, and progressive congregation made up of Washington, D.C., "movers and shakers." Gordon's journey outward in pastoral ministry and political involvement was grounded in equally strong commitment to the journey inward of contemplative prayer. "Over the years, I found what I needed in the Psalms," Gordon notes.

Today Gordon is actively involved as a congregant in a large United Church of Christ congregation in the D.C. suburbs, where he is currently serving as congregational moderator. Although he has been ordained for nearly fifty years, Gordon sees his current role in the congregation primarily as a spiritual support to the pastoral staff, and spiritual mentor to members seeking spiritual guidance. While still active in the local United Church of Christ ministerium and conference programs, Gordon sees his role in congregational life as similar to that of an active layperson.

Looking back over his five decades in ministry, Gordon asserts that his commitment to pastoral excellence could not have been actualized apart from an equally strong commitment to spiritual growth, family, and outside activities. In the midst of a demanding pastorate, Gordon found spiritual sustenance not only in the practices of prayer and contemplation but also in writing poetry and acting in community theater. Gordon has been involved in twenty-four community theater plays during his ministerial career. According to Gordon, these outside involvements kept his ministry alive and were at the heart of his personal self-care. Gordon's life is a testimony to the fact that practicing the art of excellent ministry is found in a highly intentional dynamic and evolving balance of work, study, rest, creativity, and sabbath time.

Although he has been retired from full-time ministry for nearly a decade, Gordon notes that "the hardest thing for a seasoned pastor is to be a resident retiree," especially when one remains in the same area in which he or she once pastored. Gordon asserts that healthy leave-taking involves letting go of long-term relationships and steering clear of congregational politics. It also involves leaving the congregation's future in God's hands and the wisdom of its current leadership.

As he prepared for retirement, Gordon recognized that retirement is a spiritual crisis, fraught with many dangers as well as opportunities. Recognizing that he would no longer have a regular ministerial schedule and an institutional life to support him, Gordon sought out the companionship of a spiritual director to help him to discern the shape of the first five years following retirement. Although he remains a beloved and respected pastor among his former parishioners as well as his colleagues, Gordon believes that keeping healthy boundaries is also a spiritual discipline. "When I encounter former parishioners, I am usually delighted to see them. We catch up on our lives and families. But there is one clear guideline that I bring into our encounters—I will not talk with them about Westmoreland United Church of Christ or its pastoral staff. If they begin to talk about the church or criticize its leadership, I excuse myself." His commitment to maintaining healthy boundaries has borne fruit in a positive and collegial relationship with the current senior minister of Westmoreland United Church of Christ.

Today Gordon is clearly reaping a "harvest of righteousness" in terms of his marriage, family life and relationships with his children and grandchildren, writing and poetry, mentoring of younger pastors, and commitment to ongoing spiritual renewal. The good work that God began in Gordon's life and ministry is still bearing fruit. Gordon's intentionality in joining ministry, spirituality, family, and art provided the balance he needed to respond creatively throughout all four seasons of ministry.

Something Beautiful for God

As the two of us pondered Gordon's fifty years of fruitful and in-spiring ministry, we were reminded of the words of Mother Teresa of Calcutta, who once noted that the aim of her often messy and challenging work with dying and forgotten persons was simply to do "something beautiful for God." Today, in the midst of the ever-changing demands of twenty-first-century ministry, pastors ask, "Can a life devoted to ministry continue to bring beauty to God, our congregations, our families, and ourselves?" Theologians have spoken of the beauty of holiness. In the twenty-first century, we would expand these words to affirm the beauty of wholeness, especially as it relates to the four seasons of a pastor's vocational life: (1) the sense of call to ministry and seminary that represents the springtime of ministry when discernment of call and nurture of ministerial identity are central; (2) the first congregational call, marked by adventure and tests of integrity, ordained ministry's sum-mertime; (3) then autumn, midcareer in ministry, with challenges of endurance and new opportunities for transformation; and (4) winter—retirement and the adventure beyond that require vision and letting go.

The four seasons of ministry, like the four seasons of nature, are filled with beauty for those who have "eyes to see and ears to hear." Each season has its own unique spiritual hue and opportuni-ties for growth and adventure. Still, while each season of ministry is challenging as one lets go of the old in order to embrace new ways of being and doing, each season also reflects God's personal and unique vision for one's life, congregation, and relationships. The task through all the seasons of ministry is to awaken to and embody, in one's personal and professional life, God's unique vision for the season in which a pastor finds her- or himself.

The art of ministry involves nurturing beauty and truth in the pastor's life, the congregation's life, and the world. Although we do not want to define beauty too narrowly, the two of us believe that the interplay of truth and beauty involves a dynamic and intricate ecology of diversity and unity, action and rest, community and solitude, tradition and innovation, adventure and comfort, creativity and integrity, and embracing and letting go, undertaken within the context of a living relationship with a loving, creative, adventurous, and beautiful God. Grounded in an appreciation of tradition and a congregation's or a pastor's past accomplishments, the quest for beauty and truth within ministry embraces new possibilities of creative synthesis that will bring together diverse, and often contrasting, beliefs, experiences, and persons for congregational and professional growth and transformation.

Living the Seasons of Ministry

Koheleth, the spiritual teacher of Ecclesiastes, portrays a compelling vision of truth and beauty in describing the dynamic seasons of a good life. This wisdom teacher believed that spirituality embraced the whole of life, including mortality, conflict, and failure. Wisdom and beauty are not to be achieved by avoiding life's challenges but in listening for God's inspiration and guidance within the dynamic movement of life, death, and rebirth. Listen to these familiar words from Ecclesiastes 3:1-8 as a call to prayer and reflection on the current season of your personal and professional life and its beauty.

> For everything there is a season, and a time for every matter
> under heaven:
> a time to be born, and a time to die;
> a time to plant, and a time to pluck up what is planted;
> a time to kill, and a time to heal;
> a time to break down, and a time to build up;
> a time to weep, and a time to laugh;
> a time to mourn, and a time to dance;
> a time to throw away stones, and a time to gather stones together;
> a time to embrace, and a time to refrain from embracing;

a time to seek, and a time to lose;
a time to keep, and a time to throw away;
a time to tear, and a time to sew;
a time to keep silence, and a time to speak;
a time to love, and a time to hate;
a time for war, and a time for peace.

Although the teacher recognizes that our lives are brief, "a generation goes, and a generation comes" (Eccles. 1:4), the teacher also believes that an underlying spiritual movement inspires the quest for wisdom in our mortal lives. Beauty is transitory in nature, but new experiences of beauty will emerge for those who are attentive God's presence in the constantly rising and perishing of life. The seasons come and go; and we cannot hold on to what has been. Those who listen well to the gentle rhythm of God moving through their lives and the responsibilities and challenges that attend the passing of the years, vocationally as well as chronologically, will be amazed at the beauty and truth that shapes and characterizes the development of their ministries.

Truly, there is a time and a season to every ministry. Healthy and vital pastors look for the signs of the times and the gifts of each swiftly passing season, but they also take responsibility for engaging the creative opportunities of each season of ministry. The passing of the seasons in nature or in our personal lives is never exactly the same from year to year. Just this morning, after two glorious spring days with temperatures in the seventies, the temperature dipped into the thirties as Bruce took his prayer walk amid swirling snow flurries. Indeed, there are seasons within seasons, moments that mark professional firsts, such as first sermons and funerals, as well as lasts, such as saying goodbye to a beloved congregation or giving one's final sermon before retiring from full-time ministry. To everything there is a season! Within the seasons within seasons of each ministerial adventure, the God whose creativity brings forth the seasons of growth and rest calls those of us who serve as ordained ministers to contemplate our own unique season in ministry.

The Culture of the Call

Ordained ministry has often been described as a calling or vocation. Traditional images of the call to ministry have been both good news and bad news for today's pastors. As we turn the pages of Scripture, we find inspiration and consolation in the call and response stories of biblical characters such as Abraham and Sarah, Jeremiah, Isaiah, Esther, Mary and Joseph, Simon Peter, Mary of Magdala and the women at the tomb, and the apostle Paul. Those of us called to ordained ministry take heart from stories of reluctant prophets such as Jonah, whose work bears great fruit, despite their resistance and halfhearted efforts to follow God's call to salvation. We are inspired by the promise that God will not only provide the dream of a promised land but also guidance for the pilgrimage to that promised realm.

The biblical call stories affirm that God calls persons to a variety of ministerial and congregational leadership tasks, such as preaching, teaching, healing, administration, and pastoral care. Recognizing that no *one* person can fulfill the many of tasks of congregational leadership, these call stories encourage us to explore and develop our own particular gifts. Each call is unique in its time, place, and person. Within the body of Christ, God calls persons to actualize both unique and generic gifts for the well-being of the community of faith (1 Cor. 12:4-31).

This is good news for the women and men that God calls to congregational leadership and ordained ministry. But the call to ministerial leadership often becomes bad news for ordained ministers, families, and congregations when clergy believe that their personal call is so unique that it is not recognized as an interdependent part of God's universal call to all persons within their congregations, families, and communities. As 1 Corinthians 12 rightly notes, God's call pervades the entire body of Christ. God brings forth countless gifts and talents from all persons for the common good. The call to ordained ministry is not a greater call than the call to lay leadership or other professional occupations but a specific call to commit oneself throughout one's whole life to nurturing the well-being of the body of Christ and equipping faithful ministry in its many and diverse embodiments.

While the two of us are elated whenever a seminarian proclaims words such as "God called me to ministry and I know God will make a way for me to serve God in the future," we become concerned when he or she contrasts too greatly God's call to ordained ministry with God's call within the vocational calls of carpenters, computer programmers, teachers, nurses, and physicians. We worry that such ministers will succumb to a ministerial isolationism that separates clergy and laity in the ecology of congregational life. To be sure, ordained ministers have a unique calling within the community of faith and the overall body of Christ. This calling sets before them the diverse tasks of preaching, pastoral care, teaching, and ethical integrity. Clergy are called to "equip the saints" so that laypersons may more fully experience and actualize their gifts for ministry in their homes, workplaces, and congregational life. But, at every step of the way, pastors are reciprocally nurtured and supported by a community of saints, faithful lay leaders, mentors, colleagues, and denominational officials, without which they could not labor on God's behalf.

Pastors are the spiritual children of the shaman, healer, rabbi, and prophet. They are set apart by the intensity of their encounters with the holy and their commitment to focus on God's presence in the world, as well as their education and their denominational ordination. As a result of interplay of gifts, experiences, encounters, and authorization, their ultimate vocational concern is serving God through the healing and transforming power of Word and Sacrament, continually enfleshed in personal encounters and the quest for shalom. They are blessed with the vocation of welcoming newborns into the world and standing at the bedside as companions to the dying as they prepare for the next steps of their journey.

Yes, God calls certain persons to ordained ministry. Like Isaiah, a person may respond to God's dramatic calling with her or his own, "Here am I; send me!" (Isa. 6:8). Or a mentor may challenge her, in the spirit of Mordacai's challenge to Esther, to fulfill her calling to ordained ministry for "just such a time as this" (Est. 4:14). Either way, to be healthy and creative, pastors over a lifetime of ministry, must see their calls as part of the much larger call of God throughout all creation. Meister Eckhart's affirmation that all creatures are words of God reminds us that God calls *all persons* in diverse and unique ways. Human beings are not alone in our response to God's invitation but are part of the grand ecology of call and response, which animates all creation and speaks in our spirits "with sighs too deep for words" (Rom. 8:12-27).

The affirmation of God's universal call in the church and the world is not only a theological issue but also a matter of spirituality and practice. When pastors believe that they have only *one* calling in life, they place everything else—family, self-care, friendships—in the background as relatively unimportant compared to this one, overriding call to serve God. As one pastor confessed, "In the beginning of my ministry, when the phone rang, I used to drop everything—dinner with my family, holiday activities, Little League games, and days off—sometimes for matters as small as a church plumbing problem or a cranky trustee. It took years for me to realize that by doing this, I robbed my family of a parent and spouse and I robbed myself of a life outside the church. Thank God for a colleague group that reminded me that because God is alive and active in the world and my congregation, I don't have to do everything myself."

For pastors to imagine that they have only one call in life leaves them bereft of hope and meaning when they consider what they will do when they must finally retire from full-time ministry. A seventy-five-year-old pastor, just completing his fifth postretirement interim, confessed, "Who will I be when I no longer wake up each Sunday morning ready to preach? My identity is entirely in my ministry. Everything else is an afterthought. When I lay down my robe and stole, will I recognize myself when I look in the mirror? Maybe, I'll just lie down and die!"

The two of us believe that today a new and broader theology of revelation and vocation is needed to promote and preserve healthy and creative ordained ministers. Pastors, judicatory officials, and seminary professors are challenged to take the doctrine of divine omnipresence seriously as they articulate the vocation of ordained ministry. An omnipresent and omni-active God calls persons in every moment of experience and through a wide variety of personal and interpersonal gifts. While God may draw us toward certain visions of what we can become as God's faithful followers, we must remember that healthy ministerial visions are nested within the concrete calls of everyday life. Gordon Forbes achieved excellence in ministry and integrity in his personal life because he saw God's call as multidimensional in nature. Although Gordon knew that God called him to be a pastor, he also recognized that God called him to faithfulness in marriage, parenting, political involvement, poetry, acting, writing, and spiritual direction. Today Gordon embodies the affirmation that God's call does not cease at retirement and that new life situations bring forth new callings and unceasing possibilities for ministry. Gordon is flourishing today because he sought spiritual guidance when he faced the creative dislocation of retirement. When Gordon asked, "Who will I be without the routine of congregational leadership and institutional support?" he discovered that God had new and evolving visions of his life as a poet and writer, grandparent, spiritual director, spouse, mentor, and active church member.

As we explore the many seasons of ministry with you, we pray that you will discover your own unique season of life and recognize that the shape of God's call to ministry and the intensity of the calling itself are both chronological and contextual. The texture of God's vision for a rural church pastor who is young and single may differ from the vision given to an older, suburban pastor who is married with two children. To be sure, the vocational calling of a pastor in an inner-city church in Philadelphia may be quite different than that of a pastor of an affluent suburban congregation in

Claremont, California, or that of a recent seminary graduate planting a new congregation in Atlanta, Georgia. In all ministerial relationships, context is everything, both for God and for humankind.

So too, each of the seasons of ministry provides its own unique callings. It is our hope that with forty years of ministry ahead of her, a recently ordained pastor will mediate God's graceful transformation in a form that will be quite different than those who have gone before her, and with the same integrity and commitment in creatively responding to God's call to ministry now as when she is sixty-eight years old and prayerfully planning her adventure into retirement.

Cultivating Ministry

For the past several years, Bruce has served as the director of Lancaster Theological Seminary's programs in pastoral excellence, transformation, and well-being. These programs for pastors at every season of ministry aim to support pastors by facilitating a variety of colleague groups intended for personal and professional support, spiritual formation, and continuing education in the practice of ministry. The colleague groups are for pastors in their first congregational call following seminary graduation; pastors at midcareer; and pastors considering retirement and life beyond the parish. Every participant in this program has been nominated by a judicatory official, professor, or colleague as one who exemplifies excellent ministry in her or his particular ministerial season. Inspired by the apostle Paul's affirmation to the Philippian community, "The one who began a good work among you will bring it to completion by the day of Jesus Christ" (Phil. 1:6), Lancaster Theological Seminary's Cultivating Ministry programs, supported through the generosity of the Lilly Endowment, seek to provide safe and challenging places for ministerial reflection, exploration, wellness, and growth.

Paul's words to the church at Philippi on God's good work in their lives are filled with promise, but they also inspire theological reflection, spiritual practice, and a commitment to integrity and excellence in the everyday as well as unexpected tasks of ordained ministry. The seminary hopes that faithful pastors and communities of faith will "overflow more and more with knowledge and full insight" and reap a "harvest of righteousness" in the midst of the challenges of ministry in a postmodern age through the impact of the Cultivating Ministry program (Phil. 1:9-11).

Invoked often at the colleague group gatherings, Paul's words from Philippians contain spiritual affirmations that challenge, and often surprise, pastors from every season in ministry. Following an experience of *lectio divina* based on Paul's words to the church at Philippi, a newly ordained Presbyterian pastor exclaimed, "God is doing a new and surprising thing in my life. For years, I intellectually affirmed the Reformed doctrine of divine sovereignty. But, now I know what it means in my life and ministry. God loves me and is working in all the events of my life, whether with my family or my congregation, to do something new and beautiful." On another occasion, an experienced United Methodist pastor who had been struggling with the stress of serving a numerically declining congregation saw these same words as an invitation to look toward the future with hope: "God is at work in my current congregation and in my ministry even when I don't recognize it. Though my ministry is challenging, I now see moments of grace within this congregation. I also realize that God calls me to a harvest of righteousness and will continue to bless my life, whether I stay at this church for the next few years or move on to another congregation." A third pastor, serving as a solo pastor in a Disciples of Christ congregation, heard within Paul's words the wisdom that "you can't claim a harvest of righteousness without attending to your garden. For the past few years, I thought I could do good ministry simply by my commitment to the regular tasks of preaching, worship, and pastoral care. But, I've neglected to fertilize the soil. I need to take time for prayer and retreat. I need to enroll in classes at the seminary and take time to read novels as well as well as lectionary resources. I need to go out to dinner more often with my husband and draw pictures with my son. I need to take time for coffee with friends. And, most of all, after seven years at this church, <u>I need to make plans for a sabbatical that I should have taken last year!</u>"

God is doing a good work in the lives of pastors today as they pause to cultivate their ministries and to care holistically for themselves and their relationships. While some critics note the overall decline in ministerial commitment and the pervasive mediocrity of preaching and pastoral leadership, the two of us have found the opposite to be true in our work with pastors in a variety of settings, including, but not limited to, participants in Lancaster Theological Seminary's programs in ministerial excellence, experienced pastors enrolled in Wesley Theological Seminary's (Washington, D.C.) Doctor of Ministry program, ongoing conversations and consultations with pastors throughout the United States and Canada, and spiritual direction and consultation with seminarians and clergy from a variety of denominations.

While there are pastors who fit Duke Divinity School theologian and ethicist Stanley Hauerwas's dismal description of today's minister as a "quivering mass of availability," the two of us believe most pastors are committed to excellence in every aspect of their ministry. They increasingly demonstrate an awareness of the importance of self-care and self-differentiation so that they can maintain themselves as a nonanxious presence amid the whitewater of cultural and congregational life in the postmodern era. Awareness and practice are, of course, two different things. Ordained ministry is not an easy profession, and many pastors struggle to maintain hope amid shrinking memberships and budget crises and to balance the multiple demands of their ministerial tasks, as well as to find time for spiritual nurture and healthy relationships with spouses, partners, children, and friends. Many are worn out and some show signs of potential burnout, but God is still doing a good work in their lives and ministries. Despite their congregational setbacks and the necessary loss of ministerial idealism, the two of us experience the majority of pastors as working hard to grow in wisdom, stature, and fidelity to God in the ordinary, and often repetitive, tasks of ministerial life.

A Learning Clergy

Ministerial vitality joins theology, spirituality, and practice through all the seasons of life and ministry. Pastors are the theologians and spiritual leaders of their congregations, called to share the good news in ways that address mind, body, spirit, and relationships in the concrete worlds of their congregants. The call to articulate God's presence in congregants' lives from conception to death and beyond, as well as to help persons embody the faith they affirm in congregational leadership, family life, and public service, is an all-season enterprise. It requires ongoing intellectual and theological enrichment. Whether they are progressive, reformed, evangelical, charismatic, or mainstream in theological and liturgical perspective, pastors are challenged to live and breathe their theological beliefs in the context of the surprising and challenging world of postmodern pluralism. The pastors the two of us work with don't claim to have all the answers, but they are struggling to live faithfully with God's revelation as it is mediated through the encounter with Scripture, personal experience, tradition, culture, and reason. In the course of their reflections of their own ministry, many have come to realize that a robust theology of ministry must extend far beyond narrow understandings of ministerial vocation and calling, the sacraments, and relationships between clergy and laity.

Over the past few decades, as part of the ripple effect of violations of trust through clergy misconduct, there has been a growing consensus that a life-transforming theology of ministry embraces the whole of a pastor's life and not just her or his public ministry. While they are called to ordained ministry, pastors are also called moment by moment to live faithfully and with integrity as spouses and partners, parents and friends, stewards of their own health, and caretakers of creation and society. A harvest of righteousness embraces all the arts of ministry, but it flourishes through the art of living in relationship to God's vision of our lives and the world in its entirety. Committed to spiritual growth, continuing education, and professional excellence, these pastors do not see themselves as "learned clergy" but "learning clergy," who recognize that the corporate act of ordination, like a marriage ceremony or a conversion experience, marks the beginning of a never-ending adventure in companionship with God and humankind.

Today's pastors are also called to be rabbis and spirit persons who drink deeply of the wellspring of God's presence in their lives. Many ministers not only speak of the holy in their sermons but also share experiences and practices of holiness and healing with others in the context of small group leadership and spiritual direction.

The clergy the two of us work with give evidence that the quality of a pastor's spiritual life radiates throughout her or his congregations. They know that their times of prayer and meditation as well as their living encounters with God in Scripture and in "the least of these" inspires spiritual transformation in their congregations and themselves.

A fortunate sign of postmodern times is that many of our parishioners are more concerned with experiencing God than merely talking about God. Orthodoxy alone, whether liberal or conservative, cannot give postmodern persons the lively experiences of meaning and wholeness for which they crave. The story is told of a pastor who placed a card on his pulpit that simply read, "Let them see Christ." Vital ministry today clearly is spirit-led and spirit-filled. It helps people see Christ in their own daily tasks and in their loved ones. While our treasure is always in jars of clay, today's clergy are called to develop a contagious and transforming vision of reality that is embodied in their daily spiritual practices and experiences.

In the postmodern era, vital ministry is grounded in a commitment to practicing one's faith on a daily basis. Good ministry, like good theology, is grounded in the dynamic interplay of *vision, promise,* and *practice.* Ministerial *practice* is anchored in the theological affirmation, "God in all things and all things in God." With Brother Lawrence, the seventeenth-century spiritual guide who wrote *The Practice of the Presence of God*, healthy pastors recognize that "practicing the presence" of God is the result of commitment to practicing simple everyday acts of prayer and meditation, hospitality, justice seeking, theological reflection, physical nurture, and relational care.[3] Despite the challenges of congregational life, pastors who commit themselves to a life of spiritual growth and learning that joins vision, promise, and practice will reap a harvest of righteousness in their professional and personal lives.

A Harvest of Righteousness

The four seasons of ministry find their inspiration in images of growth and harvest. Jesus's parables of the mustard seed and the sower and the seed provide a theological undergirding for vital ministry today. The reign of God is "like a mustard seed, which, when sown upon the ground, is the smallest of all the seeds on earth; yet when it is sown it grows up and becomes the greatest of all shrubs, and puts forth large branches, so that the birds of the air can make nests in its shade" (Mark 4:31-32).

The philosopher Alfred North Whitehead once described God's activity in the world as a "tender care that nothing be lost."[4] What does the life of a pastor look like when he or she believes that God is at work in the smallest of things, the most apparently inconsequential encounters and unexpected moments? What does it mean to believe that God's transforming presence is always nurturing creation towards God's vision of personal and planetary shalom? For the two of us, it means that while God's call is sometimes experienced as dramatic, God's transforming presence is most often subtle, gradual, and hidden, like the gentle growth of the mustard seed, until it bursts forth in moments of insight and clarity. Like all experiences of grace, one's call to ministry is lifelong and embraces silent preparation as well as intentional cultivation. God calls pastors to grow in ministry in every moment and season of life. New possibilities for pastoral excellence and congregational healing and transformation emerge amid the challenges, limitations, and hopes of concrete ministerial settings and personal lives when pastors commit themselves to sensitivity and awareness in ministry.

In the course of *Four Seasons of Ministry*, we will explore the meaning of God's call to a harvest of righteousness by considering the life experiences of pastors who are committed to personal growth and professional excellence. In a time in which ministry and many other traditional professions are under siege and in process of radical transformation, these pastors' lives serve as icons through which we can experience God's good work in our own lives. We lift up the lives of these pastors as models of healthy ministry and embodiments of best practices in ministerial excellence, experienced in the context of the ambiguous realities of today's ever-changing church and world. While we do not deny ministerial pathology and mediocrity, we believe that focusing on images of ministerial excellence inspires today's pastors to seek the excellence and well-being that is appropriate to their own specific congregation, personal gifts, and life situation. Accordingly, much can be learned from the well-met challenges, ideals, and spiritual and relational practices of these men and women who truly embody what is best in ministry in their own particular season of ministry and life.

When our son Matt was a young child, we learned that as parents we didn't have to be perfect, nor could we be perfect, in raising our son. We discovered that our son would flourish if we were consistent in embodying practices of "good enough" parenting and providing him with options for shaping his day-to-day activities. The same intentionality applies to the practice of ministry. A newly ordained Presbyterian pastor, Victoria, was shocked when Bruce challenged her to reflect critically upon her around-the-clock aim at perfectionism in ministry and parenting. Her approach to ministry changed when she realized that ministerial excellence did not mean perfection but "good enough" or "excellent" ministry in her unique congregation and personal context. She continues to work hard at nurturing her congregation but now leaves the harvest to God's wisdom and care. "My whole attitude toward ministry changed when I realized that I could take a day off each week, say no to unnecessary tasks, and see continuing education as part of my ministerial week rather than time off from real ministry. God's grace in my ministry meant that if I do my best to be faithful, God will take care of the rest. Today, I wake up each day with a sense of refreshment. The challenges of ministry have not gone away, but now I'm not afraid to face them, and I am learning when to let go of certain issues in order to affirm the quality of my life and ministry."

Gordon and Victoria are examples of thousands of ordained ministers who are reaping a harvest of righteousness in their congregations, families, and personal lives at their particular season of ministry. These pastors realize that although there are many paths toward excellence in ministry, a pastor who truly cares for her or his overall well-being, spiritual life, personal integrity, and professional growth will bless her or his congregation in its own journey toward faithful ministry and well-being.

Spiritual Practices for the Seasons of Ministry

Each chapter of this book integrates theological vision and spiritual practice as these relate to excellence and transformation in each of the four seasons of ministry. Cultivating spiritual practices helps pastors nurture a larger, more holistic perspective on their ministerial practice and well-being. Whether you have just experienced God's call to Christian spiritual leadership or are pondering retirement, the cultivation of a holistic perspective enables you to see both the forest and the trees in the course of your ministry.

Perspective in ministry, grounded in the quest for spiritual stature, enables pastors to experience failures as temporary and successes as an inspiration for further adventure and experimentation.

Identifying Your Current Season

Take some time to read meditatively the words of Ecclesiastes 3:1-8. As you consider the Ecclesiastes passage, in what season of ministry do you find yourself? (Your season can either be chronological or experiential in nature.) What are the joys of this season of ministry? What are the challenges of this season in ministry? What are you holding onto? What do you need to let go of in order to fully embrace your particular season of ministry?

Take time to reflect and journal on the unique season of ministry in which you find yourself. Ask God to guide you toward the harvest of righteousness appropriate to your particular season of life and ministry.

Awakening to Revelation

With Frederick Buechner, noted Presbyterian pastor and author, "listen to your life" in order to discover God in the events of ordinary life. How would you describe the quality of your spiritual awareness and personal relationships? Where are you experiencing God in your ministry today? What revelations are you receiving in your ministry and your ordinary life? Where are you experiencing God's harvest in your life today? Breathe deeply and slowly as you take time to give thanks for moments of joy, insight, and companionship in your life and ministry. (Again, you may take time to journal your response and ask for an awareness of God's continual guidance in your life.)

Finding a Quiet Center

Gordon Forbes speaks of the importance of spiritual practices in healthy ministry. What spiritual practices currently sustain you?

What new spiritual practices are you drawn toward as a means of deepening your spiritual life?

The best spiritual practices can be simple and portable such as breath prayer or what is commonly known as centering prayer. Centering prayer calms your body as well as your spirit and weaves together the many diverse tasks of ministry. Centering prayer involves the following gentle steps:

1. A moment of quiet prayer of awareness and gratitude.
2. A prayerful focus on a single image or word, such as *God, peace, joy, light, shalom, Christ,* or *Sophia.*
3. Gentle repetition of the prayer word as a means of opening to God's still, small voice.
4. A graceful response to internal or external interruptions: noticing them, letting them go without anxiety, and then returning to your centering focus.
5. After fifteen to twenty minutes of quiet centering, conclude with a prayer of thanksgiving or the Lord's (or Our Savior's) Prayer.[5]

As you will see throughout this book, centered ministry—the harvest of God's grace and a person's own commitments to spiritual wholeness—provides a good foundation for pastoral leaders to respond with care and creativity to a congregation's inevitable change, conflict, and resistance as well as to maintain personal vitality and integrity over the long haul as they practice the everyday acts of ministry.

ℂ 2 ℚ

Springtime in Ministry

Discernment and Nurture

A rabbinic midrash reflects on the meaning of God's call to Moses through the medium of a burning bush. As the story goes, when Moses was tending the flock of his father-in-law Jethro, he led his flock to Horeb, "the mountain of God." On Mount Horeb, "the angel of [God] appeared to him in a flame of fire out of a bush; he looked, and the bush was blazing, yet it was not consumed" (Ex. 3:2). In trying to understand the nature of Moses's encounter with the Holy One, the rabbis asked, "Why was the bush burning, but not consumed?" After much reflection, one of the wise ones responded, "Every day Moses passed the bush on his way to work, but never noticed it. The bush was burning, but not consumed, so that it would still be ablaze when Moses finally paused to notice it!"

While some ministers experience the call to pastoral ministry in dramatic ways and others simply know from early on in their lives that they were meant for church leadership, many pastors, like Moses, suddenly awaken to a call to ministry that had been there all along, warming their spirits and shaping their lives, but never fully noticed and, in some cases, consciously denied. When these future pastors reveal their sense of call to their own pastors, they are met with the response, "It's about time. I wondered when you'd notice."

Monica's story of her call to ministry, which she shared in Bruce's seminary study one afternoon, is similar to Paul's description of his own journey of faith: "This one thing I do: forgetting what lies behind and straining forward to what lies ahead, I press on toward the goal for the prize of the heavenly call of God in Christ Jesus" (Phil. 3:13-14).

Born in Jamaica, Monica was a mover and shaker in the world of pharmaceutical sales, training, and management before she explicitly heard the call to ordained ministry. Although her parents were not active churchgoers, she initially heard the voice of God through her grandmother's love. Her grandmother loved her unconditionally but also challenged her toward excellence in her personal and professional life. As Monica notes, "Through my grandmother's deep faith, I was able to identify a faith that allowed me to embrace the Christian faith later in life."

Now in her final year of seminary, Monica is pressing toward the goal of becoming a church planter for the United Church of Christ. Her deep faith, along with her management and organizational skills, will serve her well in the risky and challenging task of starting a new, multiracial congregation in her first congregational call. Although she was unsure what type of ministry she would seek when she entered seminary, Monica's call to church planting reflects her passion to share the good news of Jesus Christ to those who are still unaware of Christ's life-transforming power. Monica has a passion for leadership development, specifically discovering, nurturing, and empowering Christian leaders in the context of a growing community of faith. Because her skills and gifts are in alignment with her passion, Monica is destined to have a fruitful ministry.

Still, Monica was surprised when she felt the first stirrings of a call to ministry. She had been unchurched well into her twenties. When she joined a congregation in her thirties, she had held few leadership roles until she initiated a secular workshop for women entitled, "Getting Noticed without Being Drop-Dead Gorgeous." When she shared her workshop theme with friends at church, she was urged to "bring it to the pastor." In the course of adapting her workshop on self-esteem for her congregation, Monica heard a voice deep in her spirit, saying "Help them release the power that is within them." Though she recognized the spiritual origins of this inner voice, Monica pushed it into the background. After all, she was on the fast track to upper-level management with all of its perquisites—authority, status, and money.

The United Church of Christ has a motto that claims "God is still speaking," and God continued to speak to Monica in ways that would eventually lead her from the corporate world to seminary. As she became more active in her church, Monica was invited to become director of Christian education at her congregation. During the commissioning service, Monica heard God's voice once again in audible words that challenged her to "take the gospel to the world." Like the Hebraic prophets, Monica found the voice of God initially more disturbing than comforting. "How would I tell others that God spoke to me?" she asked herself. In the aftermath of her encounter, Monica felt a bit like the comedienne Lily Tomlin, who noted that "if you speak to God, they call it prayer; but if God speaks to you, they think you're crazy." In Monica's own words, they would think "I'd really lost it!"

God's call to Monica was unrelenting. "I couldn't think about anything but ministry. I was living and breathing ministry. I had trouble focusing on work. But, when I decided to go to seminary, I felt a great peace."

But the peace of God's call is lived out in the midst of spiritual and theological challenge. Monica was no exception to this creative dislocation as she explored new, and often dissonant, ideas about the Bible and Christian doctrine in seminary. Despite the cognitive dissonance she felt between the passionate faith she brought to seminary and the theological and biblical concepts she was learning, Monica embraced wrestling with her faith as essential to God's call to her in seminary life. In contrast to the emphasis on information, control, and clarity she had cultivated in the business world, Monica learned to live with intellectual and professional uncertainty and to enjoy adventure into the multivalent synchronicities and ambiguities of God's call in her life. "The mysteries of faith don't always come with black and white answers," this former Baptist notes. "I like the gray. When I opened myself to the gray, I also opened myself to new possibilities in understanding God and my vocation as a pastor."

When Bruce asked Monica what gave her direction and energy in her ministerial formation during seminary, she noted that she was a Pauline Christian, inspired by Paul's own ministry of church planting. "I hold onto the vision of church planting amid the challenges of seminary and my concerns about the risks of starting a new congregation. I often remind God that I'm forty-five and of all the things that I lack for ministry. God responds to my doubts with the affirmation, 'Yes, I know that!'" Trusting that God has planted the vision and will bring it to fruition, Monica faces the future in all its risks and ambiguity. As she looks toward the future, Monica embodies the apostle Paul's counsel to "pray without ceasing" (1 Thess. 5:17). "I pray all the time—while I'm singing, walking, or working around the house. I believe that God can speak to me at any time." For Monica, that bush is still burning and will not be consumed. "You never know when God will reveal God's self. That expectation nurtures my faith, even when I'm struggling in the present or concerned about the future." In pondering Monica's call, we can recognize God's surprising and forward-moving call within the interdependence of our lives and our faith communities.

A second-year seminarian, Aaron describes his lifelong dedication to Christ "as having Christianity in his DNA." Baptized as an infant in the United Methodist Church, nurtured in Sunday school, church camp, confirmation classes, and in the Methodist Youth Fellowship, Aaron identifies his maturing faith as similar to the gradual growth of the mustard seed. Although he can't identify a dramatic Damascus Road experience or even a datable moment of conversion, Aaron resonates with Paul's words at the Areopagus in Athens, recorded in Acts 17. "I have always lived and moved and had my being in the church and in relationship to God. From the very beginning, God was near as breath. Even when I briefly left the church in college, I still read books by C. S. Lewis, Madeleine L'Engle, and Richard Foster. Like Samuel, I was called from the womb, first, to be a follower of Jesus, and only later to begin the path toward ordination."

Aaron married his college girlfriend, Susan, two years after graduation. As they began their professional careers in the Maryland suburbs, Aaron and Susan also became active in a suburban United Methodist congregation as youth leaders and members of the young couples group. Though he aimed at a career in management, Aaron felt drawn to something more. As he observed the culture wars going on in his denomination and realized the many gifts he received in a theologically and socially diverse congregation, Aaron knew that he wanted to give something back to the denomination that had nurtured his faith and encouraged his questioning throughout his life. "As I surveyed the landscape of my denomination, I felt called to be a voice of reconciliation, someone who could find a way to bring people of diverse theological and social viewpoints together in worship, prayer, and service. Ordained ministry seemed to be the best path to following my emerging call."

No trumpets or fanfare sounded in Aaron's process of discernment. Many late-night conversations with Susan as well as solitary morning prayers prepared the soil for Aaron's announcement to his pastor of his intentions to enter seminary; his pastor simply responded, "I've been waiting for this. You have my full support and blessing."

Aaron began the process of discernment within the United Methodist Church, with the active support of his pastor, his congregation, and Susan. As a team, Susan and Aaron prayerfully explored the potential challenges of living on one salary in suburban Maryland as Aaron applied for scholarships. They conferred with other couples in which one partner had recently entered seminary and reflected on the personal and relational changes that would occur both in seminary and in congregational life. Together Susan and Aaron said yes to Aaron's call toward ministry, with the mutual affirmation that Susan's personal and professional life was also a calling from God. Although Susan continued to affirm her career in health care, they vowed that seminary would be an education for both of them. Susan would audit classes in Wesley Theological Seminary's Equipping Lay Ministry program on the weekends. They would make a commitment to praying and studying the Bible together on a regular basis. Aaron asserts that his approach to ordained ministry was grounded in the belief that "My calling is not the only one in my family. Susan has a calling, but so does everyone else in the congregation. My job as pastor is not to separate myself from the congregation, but to equip the saints for faithful leadership in the church and the world. I cannot do this alone. I need Susan and the prayers of the congregation to succeed in seminary and in the ministry to come." Susan adds, "I heard all the horror stories about couples drifting apart and even divorcing in seminary. I wanted to ensure that seminary would bring us together as a couple and as servants of God."

When asked what has sustained him in seminary, Aaron responded without hesitation, "Susan, running, and prayer." Each morning, Susan and Aaron begin the day with prayers and readings from the Upper Room and other devotional materials. Then, as Susan prepares for work, Aaron takes a twenty-minute run through their suburban neighborhood. On most weekdays, they share breakfast and the morning paper before heading to work and seminary, respectively. Aaron often listens to sermons and tapes of lectures by Christian leaders as he navigates the freeway between home and seminary.

Aaron and Susan share chores, visits to the hardware and the grocery store, and go out on cheap matinee and dinner dates every Friday afternoon. Aaron admits that the hardest thing has been to leave his home church to satisfy his seminary field education requirements. Still, he knows that the lifelong relationships and the spiritual growth he began at his home church will continue to sustain him throughout the adventure of ministry.

When Jesus called his first female and male disciples, he invited them to leave the safety of the familiar for an uncertain adventure with few signposts and little security. This was Megan's experience when she left the security of a well-established career as a middle-school teacher to enroll at Lancaster Theological Seminary. Megan had always been a seeker. "My sense of call occurred long before I said yes to ministry. I felt God's mystical presence in the intricate connectedness of things." Long before she heard the word *theology*, Megan was a theologian and mystic who had always asked big questions of the adults around her. In junior high school, Megan concluded that if God was truly loving and creative, then she could no longer accept the idea of a place of eternal pain and punishment.

Megan believed in a loving God, and yet she was no stranger to suffering. A growing recognition of the pain of childhood sexual abuse called her to go deeper in self-awareness and spiritual discovery. Although Megan never doubted God's existence, she found herself angry at God as she asked God, "Why did this happen to me?" In her time of searching, Megan found solace and direction through journaling, prayer, and artistic creations, which were inspired by Julia Cameron's *The Artist's Way*, her work with a spiritual director, and the poetry of Mary Oliver. Megan took a leave from teaching in order to discern her calling. Yet when she returned to the classroom, she continued to discern her life calling, asking, "Is this all there is to life? Isn't there something more to my life than teaching?" In her daily journaling, the word *seminary* kept popping up.

Megan's Damascus Road experience occurred at an ecclesiastical council (or ministerial authorization meeting) for a recent seminary graduate. During the meeting, which she attended as the representative of her congregation, Megan heard an inner voice whispering, "That's me. I could be her." During the postcouncil refreshment time, she went outside to work on a sermon she was to preach at the small country congregation that she attended. Synchronously, the seminarian who had just been approved for ordination stopped to chat with her and left with the question, "Have you thought about seminary?"

The moment that Megan opened her eyes to the possibility of seminary, everything in her life changed. "I felt a feeling of rightness that was accompanied by doors literally flying open for me. I felt a peace that I could not describe."

Megan describes her first year at seminary as both a joy and a challenge. A natural-born theologian, Megan has "steeped [herself] in the academic environment." "I love the questions. But sometimes I need to take a retreat just to let all the new ideas and experiences soak in." Like many other seminarians, Megan finds the avalanche of new ideas overwhelming at times. "I wish I had more time to process what I'm learning," she admits. As an INFP in the Myers-Briggs Type Indicator, she confesses "I need time to be alone, to pray, and to let the ideas swirl, and sometimes I just need to get away and to enjoy pizza with friends."

Megan, like many other gifted seminarians, is on a quest for personal and spiritual balance in her studies and in her spiritual life. She would like to have more time to integrate her studies with her growing sense of call. Megan believes that too much information, especially in the first year of seminary, can crowd out times of prayer and reflection of the sort that inspired her initial experience of call.

On Bruce's desk at the seminary is a paperweight with these words attributed to St. Augustine imprinted on it: *solvitur ambulando*, meaning "It is solved in the walking." Like Bruce, Megan is a prayer walker. She affirms, "When I walk, I feel grounded and centered." In the midst of her studies, Megan continues her commitment to journaling, artwork, and living out the creative disciplines she learned with *The Artist's Way*. Although she admits that her future is wide open, Megan dreams of creating a multigenerational community and family center that integrates arts and spirituality for personal transformation. For Megan, ministry is an artistic endeavor that brings out the inner spiritual artist in adults and children alike. As a spiritual leader, Megan wants to help Christians follow the quest to do "something beautiful for God."

It Takes a Village to Raise a Pastor

Megan's quest to find quiet times for prayer and inspiration serves as a reminder that ministry is a profoundly social profession. While solitude is essential to the spiritual formation of pastors, ministry takes root in communities of learning and discernment that often allow little time or space for contemplative prayer. Nowhere is the rhythm of solitude and community more important than in the nurture of those who have just begun the journey toward ordination.

Jesus's parable of the sower and the seed aptly describes the journey of ministry throughout its many seasons. "Listen! A sower went out to sow. And as he sowed, some seed fell on the path, and the birds came up and ate it up. Other seed fell on rocky ground, where it did not have much soil, and it sprang up quickly, since it had no depth of soil. And when the sun rose, it was scorched; and since it had no root, it withered away. Other seed fell among thorns, and the thorns grew up and choked it, and it yielded no grain. Other seed fell into good soil and brought forth grain, growing up and increasing and yielding thirty and sixty and a hundredfold" (Mark 4:3-8).

The task of faithful communities—congregations, judicatory regions, and seminaries—is to insure that the good seed of Christian leadership, growing in seminarians such as Megan, Monica, and Aaron, continues to be nurtured by providing opportunities for personal, intellectual, and spiritual inspiration and reflection for those persons for whom God's call to ministry is new, fresh, and lively. Such communities provide a context in which the initial idealism of the call to ministry can deepen and withstand the complex and challenging realities of seminary and congregational life. An environment in which the seed of call can flourish is the good soil of solid pastoral and scholarly mentoring and spiritual nurture.

Growing in Wisdom and Stature

Luke tells the story of young Jesus in the temple. In the narrative, Jesus is portrayed as so engrossed in dialogue with the temple rabbis that he forgets to rendezvous with his parents for the journey back to Nazareth. When his parents return to the temple, his mother chides him about the anxiety he caused them by his attention to faith rather than family. In a bit of theologically grounded adolescent rebellion, Jesus responds, "Did you not know that I must be in my Father's house?" The passage concludes with the comment, "And Jesus increased in wisdom and in stature, and in divine and human favor" (Luke 2:41-52).

Healthy and creative ministers are committed to growing in wisdom and stature. Many of the practices of spiritual formation, self-care, and professional leadership, essential for excellence in ministry, begin during seminary. Sadly, many of the habits that lead to burnout and spiritual dryness also begin during seminary.

The task of the seminary historically has been to nurture and shape the growing seeds of ministry into a small but healthy plant that will, in turn, grow to provide nourishment and support to a wide range of Christians and other seekers. By no coincidence the word *seminary* has its origins in the Latin word for "seedbed." A seminary is seedbed of opportunities for the spiritual, theological, personal and relational, and professional formation and nurture of pastors.

How can today's seminaries provide a healthy, challenging, and nurturing environment for the intellectual, spiritual, and practical development of persons who have experienced God's call to ministry? While there are no absolute answers to this question, in the postmodern era it is essential that seminaries and other institutions overcome the modern dualisms of mind and body, theory and practice, church and the world, tradition and transformation, and contemplation and action if they are to respond to the unprecedented social and spiritual challenges of the twenty-first century.

While the two of us do not intend to describe in great detail the challenges facing seminaries today, we would like to reflect on ways that seminaries can creatively nurture, challenge, and mentor persons whose sense of call to ministry is beginning to emerge and form. In the spirit of the parable of the sower and the seed, the seminary is challenged, first of all, to deepen and broaden the newly planted and fragile seeds' sense of call. Like the youthful Jesus, today's seminarians should be given opportunities to grow in wisdom and stature by growing beyond the parochial understandings of faith with which they may have come to seminary, thereby gaining the spiritual maturity and creative vision needed to lead congregations in a complex and changing environment and learning how to unite faith with action for the transformation of congregations and the world. Seminaries need to call their students to examine novel, creative, and even dissonant understandings of Scripture and the nature of God and the world. Then, students integrate these new insights critically in the formation of a faith that they as future pastors can affirm and preach in the complex and pluralistic postmodern world beyond seminary. This is a tall order for a seminary and its students.

To respond to today's whitewater world of change and challenge, the seminary is challenged to be "embodied"—that is, to be a place where a holistic sense of call is formed and developed in mind, body, and spirit. Practice cannot be separated from theory. The embodied seminary invites students to see their vocations and their professional lives in a holistic rather than a compartmentalized way. This is a challenge not only to professors and students but also to administrators insofar as it calls the seminary to explore within each and *every* class—whether it be a class in church administration and evangelism or systematic theology and biblical studies—the theological, spiritual, professional, and practical dimensions of every arena of ministry.

At a well-known megachurch in the Washington, D.C., sub-urbs, after Pastor Lon Solomon gives his interpretation of Scripture, the whole congregation on cue shouts, "So-o-o what!" Although this congregational response may seem a bit contrived to some of us, it serves as a reminder that there was no distinction between theory and practice in the Hebraic tradition and for Jesus, his first disciples, and the leaders of the early church. By definition, for the Hebraic tradition, all theology was practical theology uniting mind and body, theory and practice, in one dynamic synergy. Theological reflection and Scripture study was accompanied by questions similar to those contemporary Christians often ask after hearing a lecture or reading a text: Does it preach? Does it heal? Does it welcome? Does it liberate and uplift the vulnerable and downtrodden?

In the spirit of such holistic and constructive postmodern theology, theological education is at its best when it is concrete, relational, multidimensional, and lively in nature. While the play of ideas is important in shaping hearts and minds, it is clear that theo-logical reflection becomes most insightful and transformative when it occurs in lively dialogue with, and embodied within, the world of flesh and bones, communities and relationships. Paraphrasing Alfred North Whitehead's description of metaphysics, theological education begins with introspective reflection on a person's experi-ence of call as a Christian in the world, on those pivotal moments of spiritual transformation, grace, and justice seeking. Then it soars upward to envisage these transforming moments from the broadest possible perspectives of theological imagination. And finally theo-logical education returns again to the concrete world of experience to apply what it has seen and discovered to the everyday tasks of ministry and to test its theological vision in the complexities of concrete experience.[1] Conscious integration of mind, body, and spirit with the concrete realities of personal and global experience is dynamic and never ending in seminary life and in the practice of vital ministry within congregations.

Seminarians and faculty alike are challenged to think and act holistically. Often acutely aware that all subjects are dynamic and interdependent, seminarians in the process of formation must focus on the tension between the contemplation that gives birth to a global and long-term perspective and the creative agility needed to respond to concrete and swiftly moving changes in the congregation and the world. To nurture agility of mind, heart, and action, each seminary class should pause a moment for the students and even the professor to proclaim, "So what!" and wait to see what comes forth. Students and professors alike should ask, "In what ways do my theological beliefs transform my life, enable me to respond to the culture wars of this society, and heal conflict in congregations and denominations? How do my theological beliefs inspire long-term commitments to just and ecologically sound practices of witness and mission within the world?" Conversely, they must also consider, "How does all that I learn about preaching, administration, outreach, and evangelism reflect my understanding of God's action and presence in the world or in my own personal healing and wholeness?"

Hardheaded intellectuals and old-guard social activists may see this concern for seminarians' well-being in body, mind, spirit, and relationships as an example of either the triumph of the therapeutic or a softening of the self-sacrificial nature of ministry. While the two of us affirm the sacrificial and communal nature of ministry, we also believe that a seminarian or pastor must have a grounded, strong sense of self—that is, sufficient ego strength, self-awareness, and spiritual maturity—before he or she can be asked to sacrifice it. Self-giving in ministry must emerge from the true self rather than an inflated false self, works righteousness, or unhealthy codependence. Holistic spiritual formation is about growing of spirits and minds strong enough and healthy enough to sacrifice for the right things and count the cost of discipleship as they make sacrifices in their personal or professional lives.

An essential element in ministerial wholeness involves discovering the style and shape of ministry that reflects a seminarian's unique calling, nurtures her or his soul, and calls forth his or her spiritual gifts. Seminarians and their mentors need constantly to ask, What is the shape of my ministry? Where do I see my gifts responding to the church today? In what areas do I need to grow in order to integrate my spiritual gifts with the needs of tomorrow's congregations? How does my sense of God's presence in my personal life form my ministerial practice? While the gifts and passions of pastors and the needs of congregations and the church as a whole are seldom fully congruent, some minimal alignment of a pastor's deep calling with the anticipated context of her or his ministry is essential for health and transformation of pastors and congregations.

Currently, most seminarians develop practices of ministerial wholeness primarily on their own or with the counsel of a ministerial or faculty mentor or spiritual director. While ultimately the responsibility for wholeness in ministry lies with the seminarian and with the pastor he or she will become in his or her vocational life following seminary, denominational and seminary advocacy is necessary in order to promote a culture of ministerial well-being. Judicatories and seminaries must walk the talk of healthy pastoral leadership if healthy leadership is to become a priority in the church. Although seminaries and judicatories are now gradually recognizing the importance of professional balance and self-care, the two of us believe that the practices we describe in the course of this book provide a pathway toward wholeness for today's seminary students as well as pastors, both individually and as part of an emerging culture of ministerial wellness.

What Do You Do with a Burning Busy?

Dr. George Tolman, Bruce's field education supervisor at First Christian Church in Tucson, Arizona, reflected one Sunday morning on Moses's encounter with God in the burning bush. As he read over his sermon manuscript, Dr. Tolman recognized a deep truth lying in a typographical error. Instead of "burning bush," he had typed "burning busy." Thirty years later, Bruce and Kate still ruminate on Dr. Tolman's sermon title, "What Do You Do with a Burning Busy?"

Inspired by a sense of call to ministry and an experience of God, seminarians often begin seminary thinking that their days will be filled with prayer, contemplation, scriptural meditation, and leisurely theological reflection, only to discover that they have become too busy for leisurely study and quiet contemplation. As one Presbyterian seminarian ironically noted, "I was raised to practice the sabbath in my childhood home. Sabbath is still important to me, but with my classes and field education in a church, I am working every day of the week. Sabbath is the one thing I miss at seminary." An Episcopalian seminarian confessed, "When I was an aspirant, I spent an hour each day praying and reading Scripture. I still read Scripture—to pass tests and prepare for homiletics class—but I often struggle to find fifteen minutes for silence in the course of the day. Will it get any easier when I enter the priesthood?" This irony is noted by L. Gregory Jones and Kevin Armstrong in their theological reflections on ministerial practices, saying that "many clergy report that the very activities that brought them into ministry are now absent from their lives."[2] While seminary often opens new horizons and possibilities for ministerial practice, it must also build upon those spiritual practices and religious experiences that inspired students to enter the ministerial profession in the first place.

Like Lazarus's sister Martha, many seminarians are doing excellent work, but anxious about many things. Even the most intellectually and professionally gifted seminarians often complain about having too little time to play and to pray. Many go from book to book and appointment to appointment with little time for reflection and integration. In describing her own very positive experience in seminary, Monica notes that "it's not just about writing papers, but the importance of reflection on what we're learning in class in relationship to what is going in our lives and our future in ministry. We need more time to discern what God is saying through our new theological insights." Echoing Jones and Armstrong, Monica is concerned that "we try to prepare people for ministry who are not attuned to how God wants to shape and mold them for the work God wants them to do." While seminarians are called to nurture their own ministerial formation in mind, body, and spirit, Monica and other students often perceive the primary values of the seminary as academic rather than spiritual in nature. Clearly, more time needs to be spent on spiritual formation and theological reconstruction in the wake of the deconstruction students often experience in their biblical and theological courses.

For many seminarians and pastors, the primary issue is time. The importance of time for ministerial reflection was brought home to us in the responses of recently ordained pastors, now in their first congregational call, to one of their colleague group meetings. On the day of the group meeting, Bruce checked his seminary phone messages only to find that half of the group members couldn't attend because they had overbooked themselves or were running behind in their work. Ironically, the theme of the meeting was time and ministry.

Physicians say that how a person views time can be a matter of life and death. Physician Larry Dossey describes "time" or "hurry" sickness as a serious health issue for persons today. People of all ages are always on the move, always tuned in and available, whether through cell phones, e-mail, voice mail, or instant messaging. Pastors can work around the clock and dash off e-mails to congregants, secretaries, and judicatory officials at any hour of the day. Pastors certainly live under the constant cyclical pressure of the Saturday night or Sunday morning deadline for sermon preparation. The challenge to remain inspired and inspiring is quite demanding. The reality is that as soon as one Sunday's sermon is completed, he or she needs to begin thinking about the next Sunday amid the usual Monday morning avalanche of administrative, pastoral, and denominational responsibilities. The dream of becoming a scholar-preacher is illusory for most seminarians and pastors alike.

Pastors must learn to dance between *chronos* and *kairos*, the swiftly moving, linear, clock time and the spacious movement of

God's everlasting life. A major challenge in seminary and ministerial life is to awaken to God's abundant *kairos* time amid the apparent scarcity of *chronos* time.

The theory of relativity reminds us that our perspective on time may shape its passage in our lives. Ironically, the spaciousness of *kairos* time is discovered by embracing time in its dynamic movement through practices of time transformation. Traditionally, Christians have transformed their experience of time by remembering God's presence in the changing of the hours, days, seasons, and years. Following a seminar on "taking time for ministry," one Lancaster Theological Seminary student committed herself to practice sabbath rest every week. Despite his responsibilities as a father, student, part-time software consultant, and field education intern, a Lutheran seminarian, Tom, now chooses to plan ahead enough to take Saturdays off for prayer, spiritual reading, and family time. "Although there are many Saturdays I have to physically restrain myself from checking e-mail or picking up a textbook, taking time for sabbath has changed the way I look at the rest of the week. The tasks don't go away, and after church I hit the books; but, I have a sense that if I do my best, God will provide me with the time I need for excellent ministry and healthy family life." In the spirit of Jewish theologian and spiritual guide Abraham Joshua Heschel, Tom has learned that sabbath is at the heart of creation, the creation of the universe as well as his own ministerial creativity.[3]

Third-year seminarian Judith gained a new perspective on time at a weekend retreat for women in her diocese. One of the retreat leaders spoke of the ancient practice of praying the hours. Steeped in the Anglican tradition, Judith found the image of joining the monastic spirit with domestic responsibilities a life-transforming insight. Judith now integrates the traditional practices of morning prayer, vespers, and compline, found in the *Book of Common Prayer,* with silent prayer every time she hears the seminary clock tolling the hours. Judith notes that "praying the hours keeps me on track spiritually. When I take a moment to pray, I remember that God is as real right here in the midst of my day as God is in the realm of eternal life. I remember that I can catch a glimpse of eternity in the seminary library, at a stoplight, or while I'm working on a paper. Though I often forget it, praying the hours reminds me that I have eternal life right now. And, if I have eternal life with God, I really do have all the time I need to accomplish what is important in life."

Like Megan, Matt, a second-year seminarian, also experiences God's abundant time when he takes his daily midday walk. "Walking slows me down and lets my new insights soak in. Sometimes when I come out of class, my head is swirling with new ideas. But the minute I hit the college green across from the seminary, time slows down. I get my aerobic charge, but even my fast walking seems like a snail's pace compared to the rush of new ideas that I experience in every class period. I feel centered and know that even if I don't have all the answers, there is a deeper wisdom that will guide and sustain me."

This whitewater, multitasking, postmodern world requires all of us who care about our faith and health to stop and explore ways to pause, notice, open, yield, and respond to God's abundant time.[4]

The story is told of a group of Europeans traveling in an African country who employed a number of African porters to carry their supplies. After several long days of marching through the jungle, one day the African porters simply refused to move. Finally, in confusion, one of the Europeans asked them why they stopped. The head porter responded, "We've been going so fast that we needed to stop in order to let our spirits catch up with our bodies!" In seminary, students who value self-care and spiritual growth need to find a variety of ways to stop not only for physical rest but also to let their spirits catch up with the rapid pace of theological education and practical application. As students take time for prayer, rest, and sabbath, they will discover a surprising, and unexpected, truth—they will have enough to time to balance the demands of theological education and personal and relational well-being.

Mentoring and Spiritual Direction

All daily encounters have a potential vocational quality hidden within them. Every relationship can further a person's divine calling to wholeness and beauty for oneself and others if one chooses to be open to the holiness of the moment. This affirmation is not only the foundation for the initial experience of vocational call, but also the source of refreshment in every season of ministry. God is still actively calling each and every one of us. God is inspiring us even when are unaware of it! While synchronous encounters often change the course of a person's life, the growth in wisdom and stature necessary for healthy and fruitful ministry requires the ongoing nurture of intentional relationships with mentors and spiritual guides whose wise and prayerful care is constant and highly intentional.

When Bruce was in college, he was "discovered" by his pastor, John Akers. As a long-haired flower child who had left the church as a young teenager in search of spiritual experiences, Bruce returned to Grace Baptist Church in San Jose, California, the Sunday after he learned Transcendental Meditation at the Berkeley ashram. Was it a coincidence that in the course of a conversation both Bruce and John recognized that they had a mutual interest in process theology? Bruce sees in this encounter the gentle movements of divine wisdom and guidance, reflected in the call and response of life-transforming relationships. From that day on, John looked for ways he could encourage Bruce to explore the relationship between process philosophy and Christian faith. Later, John invited Bruce to teach a process theology class as part of an adult study group at the church, met regularly with him over coffee, and shared his own personal growing edges with this young, budding theologian. Inspired by a pastor and a congregation that took his gifts seriously, Bruce enrolled in Claremont Graduate University, where he found that he could serve both "Athens and Jerusalem," the academy and the church. In the nearly forty years since that time, Bruce has spent his professional life as a bivocational minister and professor, and has always flourished in his rather uniquely shaped call.

As a religion major at Scripps College in the 1970s, Kate first encountered Allan Armstrong Hunter, "walking mystic" and former pastor of Congregational Church of North Hollywood, through a lecture he gave on Mahatma Gandhi. Retired and living at Pilgrim Place in Claremont, Allan Hunter took many fledgling students such as Kate under his wing, inviting them to see themselves as young theologians and mystics on their way to spiritual leadership in the church. Allan Hunter taught the extroverted Kate the importance of silence in ministerial formation.

Bruce and Kate carry on Allan Hunter's tradition of spiritual formation every time they teach their own students a breath prayer Kate learned from her mentor in the early 1970s. "I breathe the spirit deeply in" accompanies each inhalation. In exhaling, one breathes out to the universe with the words, "and give it gratefully back again."

Allan Hunter suggested that one be as authentic as possible with how one returned her or his breath to God in prayer. If one felt anger, instead of gratitude, one was to modify the prayer to reflect her or his emotional state—"I give it angrily back again."

Hunter's unconditional positive regard of Kate and call to simple, but not pious, contemplative spiritual practices called Kate to pursue a variety of group and individual contemplative arts and mentoring not only in seminary but also throughout her pastoral career. Over the years, Kate has encountered a variety of female role models and mentors who enabled her to discover her own theological voice and articulate the unique shape of her call to ministry in healthy and creative ways.

Giving and receiving mentoring is pivotal to excellence and well-being in ministry. Monica discovered her call to ministry through her mentoring of women in the area of spirituality and self-esteem. She says that on those days when she feels like walking away from ministry, she stops and reminds herself of the harvest of righteousness in the lives of those she has mentored. On the other hand, Monica has also found that receiving good mentoring has been invaluable in her journey toward church planting in the United Church of Christ. Her field education supervisor, a church planter himself, creatively coached her through experiencing the joys and challenges of a new church start. By being able to share this experience in the growing of a new church, Monica has been able to envisage realistically the path that lies ahead for her and discern where her gifts fit in. According to Monica, a good mentor is "one who walks beside you," supporting your gifts and helping you imagine your future. A good mentor "accompanies you on your journey, stands by you in your failures, and rejoices in your successes."

Marianne found just such a mentor in an adjunct professor of theology at Wesley Theological Seminary. Her particular experience of mentoring reflects the wisdom of the Buddhist saying, "When the student is ready the teacher will come." Twice a month, following class, Marianne and her professor, a pastor-teacher, adjourned to the benches at American University to reflect on the connection between her emerging spirituality and the practice of ministry. At first, Marianne wasn't sure that she could be a pastor. "I wasn't raised in the church and I worried that my unfamiliarity with the traditional language would disqualify me from church leadership. I also worried that the Board of Ordained Ministry of the United Methodist Church would not understand my mystical orientation. Could I be both a minister and mystic?" In the spirit of theologian Nelle Morton's affirmation, her mentor "heard her into speech." Over many cups of coffee, he raised questions, provided support, and suggested alternatives. But, just as important, "he got out of the way and let me go in the direction God was calling me." This "coffee-cup mentoring" was about listening, understanding, and encouragement in finding one's own direction rather than following the mentor's unique spiritual path.

Good mentoring is a spiritual practice. It does not serve the ego of the mentor. A mentor is someone who notices the student and feels a particular empathetic affinity toward her or his spiritual journey. Mentoring is a type of spiritual midwifery that monitors the conditions through which a person's unique vocation grows; it teaches one how to manage these conditions creatively and to honor and nurture that which is growing within oneself. Mentoring is a gentle process of loving affirmation, which ultimately exists for the growth and well-being of the one who is birthing her or his divine call. To be a mentor is to selflessly let go of any preconceived images of who or what the other will become as a result of the mentoring process.

In many ways, mentoring and spiritual direction exist on a continuum. In the formation of ministers, discerning where mentoring ends and spiritual formation begins is difficult. Mentoring for ministerial formation obviously has an explicitly spiritual component, and the spiritual formation of pastors has an explicitly professional component. A third-year seminarian, Thad notes that his spiritual director regularly asks him questions such as, "Where are you experiencing God in your seminary education?" and "Toward what type of ministry is God leading you?" Another seminarian, Deborah, regularly prays for guidance with her spiritual director as she begins to circulate her ministerial information papers to various conferences and regions. Together, Deborah and her spiritual director are listening for God's guidance about where her gifts and passions might meet the needs of various congregations. When she eventually begins conversations with congregations, Deborah says that her first phone call will be to make an appointment with her spiritual director. "I know that ministry is a spiritual profession. I cannot imagine accepting a congregational call without a significant process of spiritual discernment, including prayerful conversations with my spiritual director. As we sit in silence, I know that I will discover the way that God is preparing for me." Mentoring and spiritual direction provide the nurture and protection that enable the seed to take root and deepen, far from the ravages of thorns and birds.

Habits of Wholeness for the Springtime of Ministry

On a stroll with Bruce through the verdant environment of the Franklin and Marshall campus across the street from Lancaster Theological Seminary, a second-year seminarian shared his renewed commitment to follow better health practices. "I realized that my health from now on is in my hands. Apart from a few seminars on wellness at seminary, no one has taught me to be a healthy pastor. A few weeks ago I realized that I had outgrown many of the clothes I brought to seminary last year. And I'm not alone; when I look at my seminary classmates, I notice that many of us have put on weight in seminary. I know much of it is stress related, a result of the struggles of balancing classes, field education, work, and family. But if I'm going to be a good pastor twenty years from now, I'd better make health a high priority."

Another seminarian, who like Megan regularly joins her prayer time with fast walking, notes that "every time I walk, I feel new energy and creativity. If I'm working on a paper, I notice that new ideas burst forth while I walk in my neighborhood. If I am struggling with a paper or an upcoming test, I almost always come home with a solution or a new insight." Both these seminarians embody the wisdom of *solvitur ambulando* (it is solved in the walking). The challenge these walking seminarians face is to walk early enough in the morning that the urban environment around the seminary is quiet enough for contemplative walking!

The apostle Paul captured the importance of healthy embodiment in the lives of spiritual leaders when he challenged the Christian community at Corinth: "Do you not know that your body is a temple of the Holy Spirit within you, which you have from God, and that you are not your own? For you were bought with a price; therefore glorify God with your body" (1 Cor. 6:19-20). While Paul's initial focus in these words was related to the importance of sexual morality within the community of faith, these words also apply to stewardship of the most important tool of ministry, our intricately interconnected mind-body-spirit that constitutes our lives. How pastors care for themselves as persons bears witness to their faith and spiritual commitments and profoundly shapes the quality of their ministry.

Seminarians and pastors need to ask themselves, "Do I love and care for myself as well as I love and care for my present and future congregants?" At every season of ministry, God confronts those who serve as ordained ministers with the same question Jesus presented to a man who had spent nearly four decades waiting to receive a healing: "Do you *want* to be made well?" (John 5:6, italics added). As you reflect on your need for healing, consider two questions: How important is good health to me? And, what am I willing to let go of in order to experience well-being in my professional life?

Ministry is not only relational, it is also incarnational. "And the Word became flesh and lived among us" (John 1:14). God's love for the world embraces our bodies as well as our minds and spirits. Recognized or not, bidden or unbidden, God's lively spirit flows as gracefully through our immune and cardiovascular systems as its does through our minds and spirits. Sadly, the theology and practice of ministry in which many pastors have been schooled reflects Cartesian dualism in which the relationship between mind and body are seen as a matter of indifference, if not encumbrance, for ministerial excellence. While the comprehensive Carnegie study on ministry, *Educating Clergy*, provides many insights on the theological, practical, and spiritual formation of clergy, it gives virtually no attention to pastoral well-being as professional whole-ness.[5] This omission may be more an indictment of the focus of seminary education than the authors' understanding of ministerial excellence.

According to the authors of *Educating Clergy*, "A primary task of seminary education is cultivating the pastoral, priestly, or rabbinic imagination necessary for clergy to embrace this multifaceted and public work."[6] If , as Craig Dykstra suggests, the pastoral imagination is "a way of seeing into and interpreting the world" that "shapes everything a pastor thinks and does," then a well-formed pastoral imagination must embrace the pastor's own health as well as the well-being of his or her parishioners and the theological and social context of ministry.[7] Adequate ministerial preparation must place ministerial wholeness at the heart rather than at the periphery of theological education, especially since the health of a congregation involves in equal measures the creative integration of the pastor's physical-spiritual-mental-emotional well-being with her or his theological insight and practical skill. Teaching, preaching, and pastoral care are not conveyed by disembodied spirits to disembodied spirits but involve whole persons in all their mind-body-spirit complexity.

While it is clear that persons with physical and mental disabilities and chronic and life-threatening illnesses can be effective and life-transforming vehicles of grace, there are countless instances in which neglect of physical, emotional, mental, and spiritual well-being has led to disastrous consequences in the lives of pastors and their congregations. This is especially true considering the growing incidence of ministerial burnout, stress-related illness, and misconduct among pastors as well as other professionals.

To achieve a bountiful harvest of righteousness, seminarians and pastors must clearly and intentionally take the time and energy to align themselves with God's aim for wholeness in both persons and communities. A one-sided emphasis on analysis and intellectual training of pastors leads in some instances to an imbalanced pastoral imagination that on the one hand sees everyone else's well-being as more significant than the pastor's own health and wellness, and on the other hand sees religion primarily as a matter of intellect and doctrine rather than an invigorating and creative whole-person experience.

Today's seminarians and pastors need to celebrate joyfully the incarnate presence of God and make a priority of glorifying God with their bodies. Accordingly, the two of us challenge today's spiritual leaders to choose *on their own* to make a covenant of

personal transformation along with their commitment to theological and professional excellence. This covenant begins with the small
but life-transforming step of saying yes to Christ's question, "Do
you *want* to be made well?" From that initial "yes" to well-being,
we challenge pastors to discern, in conversations with a spiritual
director, mentor, pastoral counselor, and family physician, what
practices of well-being are best suited to their health condition
and lifestyle.

This being said, beginning an exercise program is as much a
spiritual as a physical issue. Consider this humorous bit of information that while the regular practice of jogging, over a lifetime,
will add at least a year to a person's life, most joggers spend nearly
a year of their lives jogging. Let there be joy in your exercise program, whether it be walking, swimming, jogging, dancing, pilates,
or yoga.

While the challenges of life are solved in the moving, answers
are also nurtured in rest. To everything there is a season—a season
to work and a season to rest. While each person is unique, the image
of sabbath reminds us that doing nothing is just as essential to well-
being as exercise. Without sleep, a person cannot dream; without
sabbath, the well-spring of divine energy and insight necessary for
excellence in ministry will eventually dry up.[8]

Life is also nourished in the eating and drinking. Bruce humorously tells of the story of visiting five farm families in his rural
congregation and being served a piece of apple or cherry pie and a
cup of coffee at each visit. He remembers that he barely survived
the journey home to teach his evening course at Wesley Theological
Seminary! While the words "you are what you eat" are not to be
taken literally, nevertheless, how and what a person eats is essential
to her or his personal, relational, and professional well-being.

Although many theologically liberal pastors identify prayer at
meals with an outmoded ritualism reflecting the conservative faith
they left behind in childhood, eating with a prayerful attitude con-
nects us not only to the gifts of God but also to those who labor to
produce our food and those creatures who give us daily sustenance.

In our own home, we strive to see meal time as holy time, similar in kind to the eucharistic feast. We eat together as a family as much as possible and keep the table clear of work as much as possible. In this spirit, we suggest that every pastor have caller ID. In our household, when the phone rings during our mealtime, we check to see if it is from our son, his wife, or someone whom we believe may be in crisis. But beyond that, our meals are sacred and not to be interrupted. Meals provide an opportunity simply to be with one anther in a nurturing way. Compared to watching the news or reading the paper during meals, we find that sharing a story from our daily adventures, gazing together at the colorful repast set on the table, or contemplating the woods behind our home as we enjoy eating the evening meal is a gift.

What you eat is essential to your pastoral well-being as well. Take time to practice mindful eating in the spirit of the psalmist's counsel, "Taste and see that God is good." Taste the food that you eat. Does it truly taste good? How do you feel after you eat? Does it cause to have more or less energy? Are you joyful or depressed? While there is no *one* diet for all persons, we suggest that, in conversation with a nutritionist or physician, you consider a balanced diet of fruits, vegetables, juices, water, dairy products, and modest portions of fish, meat, and fowl. Our preference is for unprocessed and locally grown organic or natural foods that increase your energy and vitality immediately and over the long haul. In addition, there is a close correlation between a healthy diet of locally produced, simply and minimally processed foods and a just and sustainable approach to economics.[9]

Recognizing that many congregations run on a staple of doughnuts, pies, and cakes, we suggest that you can indeed balance politeness with healthy eating habits. This may be especially difficult at traditional potluck dinners where the cooks are often on the lookout to see what the pastor eats and whether or not the pastor samples the cook's home-cooked dessert or lasagna. Kate made a significant pastoral faux pas when she brought her prepackaged Jenny Craig diet dinner to a congregational potluck dinner. The situation was socially awkward enough that at the next potluck dinner, she challenged herself to eat by the practice that we taught our son when he was small, taking a "no thank you helping."

What a joy it is to develop and maintain a healthy incarnational ministry that glorifies God in its embodiment and rejoices in the gifts of all the senses. Divine revelation comes through taste and touch as well as sight, sound, and smell. Clergy can lead the way in their daily practices of self-nurture and hospitality.

Spiritual Practices for the Springtime of Ministry

The following activities offer ways for you to nurture your mind-body-spirit.

Breathing Lessons

One of Baltimore author Anne Tyler's books is entitled *Breathing Lessons*. While life and ministry are impossible without breath, many of us have forgotten the simple gift of mindful breathing. Sometimes the most important spiritual practices are the simplest and most accessible. This exercise can help you explore the wonder of breathing.

Take a moment to simply breathe. Experience the joy of inhaling and exhaling. How would you describe the quality of your breath? Is it deep or shallow? Let yourself take a large breath, letting your belly rise with each inhalation. How does it feel to inhale with a sense of intentionality and care? Breathe again. Can you feel the warmth and relaxation sweeping through you?

Mindful breathing can center and calm you in times of change and stress. Bruce advises his seminary students to take moment to breathe deeply before they launch into preaching their sermons. As you come to the pulpit, take a moment to arrange your papers and let yourself breathe deeply; imagine your whole being filling with

God's love and light. Breathe out any anxiety or fear. Then begin your sermon, while remaining centered in God's holy breath.

This same breathing practice can calm you in times of conflict or anxiety. In the course of a church meeting when voices are raised in contention, take a moment to be still. If it is appropriate, invite the participants to join you in a moment of quiet breath prayer. Instead of entering the fray, breathe deeply from God's still point in your life. Open to divine inspiration as you inhale. As you exhale, let go of the need to be "right." Better yet, invite your church leaders to see meetings as spiritual activities, surrounded and permeated by an attitude of prayer.

The breath prayer Kate's mentor Allan Armstrong Hunter taught her can be practiced at any time and place. With each inhalation, simply say to yourself the words, "I breathe the spirit deeply in." As you exhale, you may choose to send forth gratitude or let go of stress or anxiety by saying, "I give it gratefully out again."

Taking Time for Sabbath

A person's perception of time can be scarce or abundant in nature. Sadly, too many pastors run on scarcity. Although God has given us abundant life, pastors running from meeting to meeting and task to task without any spiritual pattern run the risk of burnout. Constantly checking their watches, keeping track of how much time they can give to their children, partner, or person in need, they live by *dead*lines instead of *life*lines.

Periodically stop to explore how you live "the time of your life":

- What do you spend your time on?
- Do your activities reflect your values?
- What do you need to do to embrace and experience more abundant life?
- What activities do you need to drop in order to experience time as abundantly full and spacious?

- What *life*lines can you set for yourself and who can help you stay accountable to them?

Consider experimenting with various spiritual practices that transform your experience of time. For example, you may choose to pray the hours. If there is a bell tower or grandfather clock nearby, let each hour's passing call you to a simple breath prayer, accompanied by a word or gesture of gratitude, petition, or intercession. Whether or not you come from a liturgical background, you may also choose to take a few minutes throughout the day to practice the traditional prayers found in the *Book of Common Prayer,* such as the offices of morning prayer, evening prayer, vespers, and compline.

As you reflect on how you spend your time, consider taking a generous period of time each week for sabbath as a way of receiving the bounty of the universe and resting in God's care. While there is no *one* way to practice sabbath, you might commit to taking a break from sermon preparation or program planning in order to devote yourself to friends and family, devotional reading, or spiritual rejuvenation. Another way to observe a deepening of time is simply to refrain from sending or receiving e-mail for a day or half-day each week.

Perhaps one of the most radical acts of trust in God's abundance involves taking off your watch or cell phone timepiece in order to simply observe the flow of time from one event to another. While watches and clocks are essential to a life involving meetings and appointments, freedom from the clock reminds you that timepieces are your servants and not your masters. Sabbath time "neither toils nor spins" in its trust in God's generous care for the universe and your life.

Solvitur Ambulando

"It will be solved in the walking." Experiment with a gentle exercise such as walking, or if you prefer, swimming or jogging, in which you can simply let go of any agenda other than the practice of noticing your body, the environment that surrounds you, and the thoughts or feelings that flow into your experience. For Bruce, walking joins reflection, prayer, study, and exercise. He often advises and mentors students or spiritual directees on his peripatetic journeys. As mentioned before, the two of us also walk together at least once a day. Movement opens us to new ways of looking at our lives and allows new insights to flow from the unconscious to the conscious mind and from person to person, gazing in the same direction.

A Covenant of Spiritual Transformation

In the spirit of the developmental spirituality of James Fowler, as pastors progress through one season of ministry to the next, they still need to nurture the gifts of the previous season. Springtime in ministry calls pastors to discernment and self-nurture, to listen well to God's presence in their lives and make a commitment to developing their own unique gifts for ministry. Whether you are exploring the call to ordained ministry, a seminary student, or a pastor in one of the later seasons of ministry, we invite you to consider making a covenant of transformation for the springtime of ministry. Adapt this covenant to your own unique life situation, gifts, and personality type.

The covenants of springtime in ministry might include the following vows you make with yourself and God. Practiced regularly as affirmative statements, covenants can focus and transform your mind, eventually enabling you to embody new behaviors and perceptions of reality.

- I covenant to listen for God's voice in my own experience, in times of prayer and meditation, and in all the encounters of my life.
- I covenant to nurture the gift of ministry by committing myself to practices of ministerial well-being and ongoing theological education.
- I covenant to take Sabbath time each week for rest, study, and family life.

❧ 3 ❧

Summertime in Ministry

Adventure and Integrity

Launching out into one's first pastoral ministry following seminary can be disappointing and daunting as well as exciting and adventuresome. In his narrative of his first few years in congregational ministry, Duke Divinity School professor Richard Lischer describes his initial glimpse of the rural church that would eventually become his first congregational call following graduation from seminary. As he gazed upon the church and the adjoining parsonage, Lischer recalls that "I felt something flop in my stomach. Then a crushing sense of disappointment. So this is what has been prepared for me, I thought, as if something should have been there for me."[1]

Another newly ordained central Pennsylvania pastor, Craig, noted that when he first arrived at the congregation he was to pastor, he had an experience similar to one Lischer describes in *Open Secrets*: no one was there to greet him! He and the chair of trustees had somehow confused the date of his arrival. Later, he noted that "as I tried to secure entrance into the deserted church building, I prayed that the people would be more open to me than the doors of the church. I tried to recall all the important things I had learned about congregational life in seminary. I knew that I had a good foundation for ministry. But, at that moment, I drew a blank. I was single, on my own, with no safety net. With fear and trembling, I prayed simply for wisdom and guidance, and—more importantly—survival, as I surveyed the deserted church grounds. Though it has been a good fit for me to pastor this church, I must admit that nothing in seminary prepared me to jimmy open a locked parsonage door!"

In looking back at his installation as pastor of that rural Lutheran congregation, Lischer, like so many other newly ordained ministers, recalls the incongruity between the immensity of pastoral tasks that lay ahead of him and his lack of practical experience in ministry. "My parishioners were expected to welcome an inexperienced twenty-eight-year-old stranger into a community as tightly sealed as a jar of canned pickles. The church had decreed that henceforth I would be spiritual guide, public teacher, and beloved sage with a stroke of a wand. God—or the bishop—had just made me an expert in troubled marriages, alcoholism, teen sex, and farm subsidies."[2]

A recently married associate pastor expressed this same tension between experience and expertise. "People come into the church office each day of the week expecting me to provide guidance on breastfeeding, child rearing, responding to rebellious teenagers, and supporting aging parents. Sometimes all I can do is pray—for myself and for them!" She adds, "Being a pastor is often a useless profession—dealing with problems that can't be fixed. But then I remember that I all can do is listen and pray, and at such times that is enough." As such moments of insight indicate, many newly ordained pastors know deep down that, despite their inexperience, God will continue the good work that God has begun in their lives and ministry. But, unfortunately, others do not have this assurance of faith and self-confidence.

Much depends on the consolation and guidance of the cloud of witnesses that have gone before them. Regardless of their view of biblical inspiration, new pastors can find inspiration in the call stories of Scripture, when they recall that the great heroes and heroines of biblical spirituality all experienced God's calling as greater than their resources and training. Isaiah protests his moral inadequacy before the God of the universe and then stammers yes to God's call. Peter protests his previous occupational and moral failures and then follows Jesus into a new vocation. Mary expresses her amazement to the angelic visitor and then opens to the surprising birth God has in store for her. Whether he or she is twenty-five or fifty-two years of age, virtually every new pastor can identify with Jeremiah's response to God's call to be prophet and preacher to a wayward people. "Then I said, 'Ah, Lord God! Truly I do not know how to speak, for I am only a boy'" (Jer. 1:6). Each one hopes to hear a word of confirmation that will enable her or him to respond creatively to the challenges of a ministry for which no one can fully prepare. "Do not say, 'I am only a boy'; for you shall go to all to whom I send you, and you shall speak whatever I command you. Do not be afraid of them, for I am with you to deliver you, says the Lord" (Jer. 1:7). The hope of each new pastor and every pastor throughout the seasons of ministry is that the God who presents them with a vision and calls them into a vocation will provide them with the inspiration, courage, and energy to embody God's dream for their lives in all of life's complexity and uncertainty. And the evidence of pastoral experience suggests that, on the whole, God does.

An Adventure of Firsts

Transition is the essence of life. The birth of each moment emerges from the death of its predecessor. Transformation always means the deconstruction of the familiar as the foundation for adventure and creativity. And so it is in the transition from seminary to full-time congregational leadership.

This transition involves gain as well as loss. With little or no experience in ministry, newly called pastors at twenty-five and fifty-five now carry the weight of congregational leadership, pastoral care, and strategic visioning. The pastoral imagination cultivated in seminary must now be concretized in the everyday tasks of ministry in all their joy and challenge. Once passive learners in seminary, new pastors must now actively lead and claim the authority that God, seminary education, spiritual experience, and the congregation have given them. They must claim their own preaching voice and their own listening ear. As one recently graduated, ordained minister shared, "I feel like I don't have the excuse of being a student anymore if I make a mistake."

Among the many firsts virtually every new pastor experiences in the adventure of congregational ministry is feeling unworthy or unqualified as she or he faces the first funeral and the delicate process of weaving together grief counseling, funeral service planning, and responding sensitively to family and congregational dynamics of grief and loss—all in a three-day period. New pastors encounter their first funeral with fear and trembling, worried that something will go wrong, that they will make an unforgivable pastoral or liturgical blunder and re-wound the already suffering congregants. One new pastor recalls that she was so nervous as she read the narrative of the raising of Lazarus that she failed to notice that the church secretary had typed John 11:39 rather than John 11:25 in the funeral bulletin. Instead of reading "I am the resurrection and the life," she launched into, "Lord, there is already a stench because he has been dead four days."

Once in a ministerial lifetime—and even in one's first few months as an ordained pastor—there comes the challenge of a memorial service for a family in the midst of the shock of suicide or after a national disaster such as the attacks of 9/11. At such moments, as inexperienced as he or she may be, a newly ordained pastor must summon the power to heal and to reassure that is her or his inheritance as a minister of the gospel.

Yes, the transition from seminary to congregational leadership is an adventure of "firsts," whether these involve leading worship for the first time without a mentor, preaching the first Lenten sermon series, or mediating the first conflict among youth group leaders or church school teachers. Every pastor remembers that her or his first baptism, whether by sprinkling or immersion, was filled with a sense of joy at welcoming a new Christian into the family of faith and a sense of relief that both the baptized and the pastor survived the process without physical injury to one or professional embarrassment to the other.

Most pastors eventually encounter—and discover they will survive and learn from—their first pastoral "failure." A well-prepared and brilliant seminary graduate, already beloved by her congregation, recently confessed that she forgot to visit one of the church's matriarchs both while she was in the hospital and during the first week of her recovery at home. This usually careful and well-organized pastor was mortified. All she could say was "I'm sorry" when she finally mustered the courage to visit the matriarch at her home. Happily, she had learned early on in her ministry that her calling was to be good enough and not perfect as a pastor and that the church is a "hospital for sinners, and not a memorial for saints," including their pastor.

The adventure of firsts ought to call every new pastor to remember that he or she cannot be a lone ranger in congregational ministry. Getting through the firsts with grace and effectiveness is best accomplished with the counsel of an experienced pastor and the prayers and support of a group of peers in ministry. While each pastor must come to the pulpit or the graveside on her or his own, the counsel and support of others serves as a protective and guiding cloud of witnesses and a reminder that he or she will survive the rough and ready frontiers of congregational leadership. Also, realistic expectations and preparation make up the solid, practical foundation for embodying the arts of ministry from day one in a pastor's career.

All transitions bring anxiety to the pastor, to her or his family, if he or she is involved in a committed relationship, and to the congregation. Even if the new pastor were to preach word for word from the text of a beloved predecessor, he or she would still arouse anxiety in the congregation simply because people are hearing a new voice at the pulpit. While these times of anxiety can be unsettling for pastor and congregation alike, they may also create the context for the creative dislocation from which God's surprising grace emerges.

When Kate made the transition from associate to senior pastor, regular lunch meetings with a seasoned senior pastor colleague helped her stay calm through many potential crises in ministry. There is no better way to sustain being a nonanxious presence in ministry than through the companionship and counsel of wise colleagues. In every season of ministry, healthy collegial relationships will give a pastor a sense that she or he is not alone and that help is on the way when the challenges of ministry become more daunting than exciting. With the companionship of colleagues and their own commitment to healthy spiritual and personal practices, pastors in the summertime of ministry will discover that God is with them in the transitions.

Every time of change is a wilderness experience for the pastor and the congregation alike. The new pastor, like the children of Israel, newly liberated from Egypt, may long for the predictability and comfort of seminary life. She may ask, feeling depleted after an especially unproductive board meeting, "Why did I ever leave seminary to come to this place? Have you led me here, God, simply to leave me alone and without resources?" Yet, as the exodus wilderness story proclaims, God guides us even when we are unaware of it. The biblical witness tells us that manna and quail, coming in the form of helpful, caring colleagues and divine inspiration, is always available, even in the wilderness of ministry, for those who open their lives to God's creative presence moving in all things. In that liminal time, the "in-between time" in which the path ahead is unclear, new pastors need to reach out and train their spirits to see deeply into God's vision for this time in their lives, and in the congregation's, by committing themselves not only to prayerfulness and devotional reading but also to companionship with peers and mentors.

Integrity in Ministry

Jackson Carroll, Duke Divinity School emeritus professor and director of the Pulpit and Pew project, notes in his book *God's Potters* the complaint of one overworked pastor: "Being in ministry is like being stoned with popcorn . . . you know, it's just one little thing after another until you feel buried in it."³ No two days are alike in pastoral ministry. The novelty of ministry and the many skills it demands, many of which can only be learned on the job, may lead either to fatigue or to vitality. On the one hand, the multitasking required of today's pastors may lead to the lament of a sixty-nine-year-old Roman Catholic priest, "I go to bed tired, and wake up still tired."⁴ On the other hand, it may lead to the sheer excitement that one recently ordained pastor experiences as he awakens each morning with the questions, "What new thing will happen today? What challenges will I face? Where will I see God in the nursery school, the church office, or the hospital room?" While the cynic in us murmurs, "Just wait" to such exuberance, we know that each day in ministry brings opportunities to serve God.

Vitality that undergirds spiritual disciplines enables pastors to encounter each new task with what the Buddhists describe as the "beginner's mind." Lively ministry is also a matter of intentionality and discipline, which give pastors a foundation for creatively facing the unexpected and the uncontrollable nature of life. With Reinhold Niebuhr, new pastors can rejoice in the many tasks of ministerial excellence:

> Granted all the weaknesses of the church and the limitations of ministry as a profession, where can one invest one's life where it can be made more effective in many directions. . . . Here is a task that requires the knowledge of a social scientist and the insight and imagination of a poet, the executive talents of a businessman and the mental discipline of a philosopher.⁵

As one recent seminary graduate noted, "I was surprised how much there is to do in parish ministry. Sometimes the unending repetition from week to week wears me down, but at other times, it exhilarates me!" While most ministers survive "being stoned by popcorn," the fact is that many pastors also flirt with "brown out," if not burnout, over the course of their ministries.

Excellence in pastoral ministry joins the gifts of both Mary and Martha, a committed willingness to seek first God's reign while giving attention to the mundane and practical details of ministry. Because God is in the details, pastors do not need to sweat the small stuff in ministry, but neither can they ignore it. Once again achieving balance is the key to ministerial vitality over the long haul. Without the commitment to doing ordinary things in an extraordinary way, exemplified by Martha at her best, Mary's contemplation becomes "so heavenly minded that it's no earthy good." But, without Mary's commitment to stillness before God, Martha's task-oriented ministry leads to perfectionism and anxiety. As a pastor in one of Lancaster Seminary's Wholeness in Ministry colleague groups admitted, "I seem to go from one task to the next with little time for reflection or prayer. I need to see the big picture in order to find my bearings. Before seminary, I prayed and exercised two hours a day. Now, fresh out of seminary and in my first congregation, I'm lucky if I pray ten minutes each morning and exercise twenty minutes, three times a week. I need to make a commitment to pray more and walk more so that I can discern what's really important in my ministry today." In the words of the late Charles Hummel, former president of Barrington College, this pastor is taking the first steps in finding "freedom from the tyranny of the urgent."[6]

Excellent pastors in the summertime of their ministries learn to find joy in ordinary tasks of ministry, bringing a spirit of celebration to their vocations that will permeate board meetings and youth group leadership as well as Sunday worship. While the task of seminary is to fertilize and deepen the soil within which the seeds of ministerial excellence, fidelity, and creativity can grow, the task of the first few years of ministry is to nurture integrity and adventure by protecting the tender shoots of ministry from the onslaught of predators, such as nonstop multitasking, that threaten to devour one's sense of joy and purpose. To do this, clergy in the summertime of ministry must make a commitment to wholeness in every aspect of their lives and ministry.

Integrity and Authority

Today's pastors are the spiritual children of the ancient shaman whose task was to mediate the power of the spirit world to everyday life. In that spirit, they also are called to share the teaching, healing, and preaching ministry of Jesus of Nazareth as he mediated the power of God's spirit to the everyday lives of those who followed him. What does it mean for pastors to claim the calling of being revealers of the sacred and "conduits for the power and wisdom of God to enter the world?"[7] While it may seem like a tall order for any pastor making the transition from seminary to her or his first congregational call, parishioners—whether they support or resist their pastor's theological viewpoints, pastoral leadership, or spiritual care—deep down expect her or him to have a certain intimacy with God and intimate self-knowledge so that their spiritual leader can speak God's truth in times of crisis and uncertainty. Developing emotional maturity is only one small part of such a responsibility.

One pastor recalls that just a month after beginning his first congregational call, the nation was shocked by the terrorist acts of 9/11. With only two pastoral care classes and one preaching class behind him, he felt ill-equipped to reassure young children and comfort their parents. "They wanted to know that there was something dependable in a world gone mad, and they wanted someone, even a wet-behind-the-ears pastor, to tell them that God's love was more powerful than terrorist attacks." So, with fear and trembling, he scrapped his prepared text and liturgy and preached from the heart on Psalm 46 and Romans 8:38-39. Six years later, members still remind him of that Sunday when they sang "A Mighty Fortress Is Our God" and heard convincingly God's words of reassurance in the halting message of a young preacher, "Nothing—not even a terrorist attack—can separate us from the love of God in Christ Jesus our Lord." One doesn't have to be a Pentecostal to learn to trust the Spirit of God to provide, if we only listen to it in times of need.

As spiritual children of the shaman and prophet and bearers of Christ's good news, new pastors are given and, in fact, have an archetypal authority well beyond their experience. Like hospital medical residents barely out of medical school but now called doctors, new pastors have prepared to respond to spiritual crises, questions of faith, and intimate secrets on a moment's notice. A call in the night sends them to the hospital to a family waiting in the emergency room to hear whether a parent will survive a heart attack or a teen a car accident. The pastor's job, therefore, begins with the discipline of practicing the presence of God in the ordinary tasks of ministry so that he or she may fully respond to be present pastorally, as needed.

Although authority is always contextual in nature, Jackson Carroll captures the essence of pastoral authority as "the right to exercise leadership in a particular group or institution, based on a combination of qualities, characteristics, and expertise that the leader has or that the followers believe that he [or she] has." Carroll asserts that our authority as pastors is ultimately relational and grounded in the perception that we are "reliable interpreters of the power and purposes of God. . . . This involves both spirituality and expertise, not one without the other."[8]

While new pastors can take solace in their faith that God has called them to proclaim the gospel and has sustained and inspired them during their seminary preparation, in tandem with the decisions of judicatory officials and congregations that called them to ordained ministry, still most new pastors struggle with the meaning of authority in the postmodern world. "I know I must be a visionary and leader for this congregation," one new pastor confessed, "but I am still struggling to articulate my own images of God, the scope of salvation, and the nature of pastoral leadership." Many pastors would echo the confession of this pastor trying to build a bridge between what she learned at seminary and her parishioners' understandings of God. "Sometimes I am tempted to shelve what I learned at seminary and simply preach the lectionary without bringing in issues such as the nature of God, theological diversity, and biblical criticism. Yet, I realize that if I hide my theology, I will lose my passion for preaching. Right now, I'm learning how to share my own vision of faith in such a way that they can gradually see the importance of new visions of God and humanity."

Pastors are the theologians of their congregations, and living up to this responsibility requires courage, creativity, and care as well as serious study and continuing education. As long-time pastor and counselor Jack Good notes in the *Dishonest Church,* recently ordained as well as experienced pastors will soon experience professional "brown out" if they simply try to reflect the congregation's spiritual values, cultural mores, and theological standpoints while hiding their own understanding of the faith.[9] As Reinhold Niebuhr once counseled, pastors are called to "agitate the comfortable, and comfort the agitated."

Relational authority must be both flexible and defined. In a changing world, congregations need self-differentiating leaders and pastors more than process facilitators. While many pastors appropriately embody a listening and facilitative approach in their leadership style as they seek to discern God's voice in the voices of their congregation, eventually all eyes are on the pastor when a member of the board asks, "Pastor, how do you think we should spend the benevolence fund?" or "Pastor, should children be allowed to take communion?" At such moments, parishioners need a theologian and spiritual leader who will share his or her vision without demanding agreement.

Many new pastors in the United Church of Christ faced this challenge of comforting the afflicted and afflicting the comfortable "writ large" following the 2005 General Synod's affirmation of marriage equality. Like several other pastors Bruce advised in the wake of the General Synod, Todd recalls the chair of the consistory pulling him aside after church with a question that raised all of his fight or flight responses. "A lot of persons in the congregation are upset about the Synod's decision and want to vote to leave the denomination. What do you think about homosexuality, pastor? Should we have a vote on this?" Todd admits that "nothing in my seminary education prepared me for that moment—to be a theologian, ethicist, expert in polity and church order, and calm and reconciling presence all at the same time. I knew that this was a defining moment for my young ministry. So, I said a brief prayer and breathed deeply and reminded him that Synod decisions were not binding on congregations, that although I had no plans to perform a same-sex marriage in the church, I was also a loyal member of the United Church of Christ and would oppose any vote to leave the denomination." Todd's gentle act of self-differentiation, of sharing his vision while maintaining his pastoral relatedness, repeated several times over the next few months, was an important step in a congregational conversation that allowed members to speak their minds, express their diverse viewpoints, and know that they had been heard by their pastor and fellow congregants. Today, although Todd's church is not "open and affirming" in terms of marriage equality, it proudly displays the United Church of Christ banner, "God Is Still Speaking" and has maintained its financial support of the denomination.

While all pastors receive some authority as a result of their education, ordination, and congregational function, the fact is that pastoral authority is ultimately grounded in the ancient virtues of spiritual experience, fidelity, embodied love, and consistently demonstrated competence in the arts of ministry, which are preaching, teaching, pastoral care, spiritual guidance, and administration. One earns a congregation's trust over time. If it is true that a new pastor operates largely within the residual shadow of expectations from the previous pastor for four to five years, then, clearly, patience and fidelity in ministry over an extended period of time are needed to build authority for prophetic leadership.

Therefore, "be prepared" is an appropriate motto for both scouts and pastors. Lack of preparation is one of the few unforgivable sins pastors commit, according to parishioners. As one church patriarch noted, "I give my pastor a little slack during Advent, Christmas, and Holy Week, but I still expect him to be punctual and ready to give his best efforts in every meeting, except when there's an emergency. I expect the same expertise and preparation from my pastor as from my physician even during a tough week. I'd rather he'd cancel the meeting than waste my time or show up with nothing to say." Another layperson echoes this sentiment, "I know my pastor is busy, but so am I. If I show up on time and prepared, I expect the same thing from her."

Excellent pastors need to prepare for and anticipate the unexpected, much like emergency medical personnel. As one commentator on ministry has noted, the interruptions and emergencies are the stuff of Christian ministry. As we will discuss later in this chapter, high-functioning pastors recognize that although they cannot manage time due to the unexpected surprises of ministry, they can regularly use quiet days, continuing education opportunities, and moments for rest, self-care, and family time to nurture excellence in the many tasks of ministry.

Integrity as Vision

The biblical tradition proclaims that without a vision, the people perish. Without a vision for one's flourishing, personally and professionally, ministry becomes captive to the tyranny of the trivial and the whims of parishioners, just as, without a vision, congregations stray from their vocation as communities of hospitality and healing. Bickering, nit-picking, and dissention replace the quest for shalom—healing and wholeness and "the peace that passes all understanding."

Like most pastoral virtues, visionary ministry is a matter of spiritual practice, creative imagination, and disciplined intentionality. Healthy pastoral authority is grounded in the pastor's understanding of the church and its mission, the nature of God's activity in the world, one's particular gifts and limitations, and the vocation and expectations of the ministry to which he or she is called.

Pastoral ministry is profoundly theological. Although postmodernism reminds us of the limitations and relativity of every doctrinal position, pastors must still live by and be able to articulate a "good enough" vision of God and human life to hold their own integrity while leading others. While theology is often accused of being abstract and unrelated to the tasks of concrete life, pastoral and theological imagination guides and informs virtually everything pastors do. A pastor's philosophy of life enables her or him to prioritize the many tasks of ministry, support a congregation's articulation of its vision and mission in the world, and gain perspective of the "forest and the trees" amid congregational decision making and conflicts. Having a clear but growing vision of God enables pastors to experience hope and provide guidance in responding to crises, whether of the magnitude of terrorist attacks, the death of a child in the congregation, a budget shortfall, or controversies related to judicatory level prophetic decisions. An ongoing commitment to engaging the truths of Scripture and the most insightful contemporary and classical theological writings through individual and group study enables pastors to speak a word of reassurance when the foundations of congregational and pastoral lives are shaken by death and destruction. This same commitment to theological reflection enables pastors to preach vital and inspiring sermons and to lead liturgies that have depth and gravitas week after week.

Most clergy know that you cannot conjure depth of thought from a fifteen-minute glance at online lectionary resources or inch-deep theological reflection cribbed from a Sunday school curriculum. A regular commitment to study is essential for the faithful improvisation necessary for excellent ministry. Jazz musicians can improvise precisely because they have an intimate knowledge of and a flexible relationship to music theory, the limits and possibilities of their instrument, and their own limits and possibilities. The same is true for ministry. Practicing theology on a regular basis brings wisdom to the concrete acts of ministry. A spacious and lively mind, able to entertain diverse understandings of God's presence in the world, church doctrine, and congregational excellence, is the result of time intentionally spent dedicated to study and reflection.

To be a professional means to be guided by one's deepest beliefs. While few seminary graduates have a fully formed theological framework, the quest for excellence in ministry requires pastors to have a witness and a vision, even though they still may be forming, that can be shared in preaching, worship, teaching, spiritual care, and administration. In the marketplace of spiritual practices and religious traditions, parishioners want their pastors to believe something and share something, even if it is provocative and challenging.

By their commitment to ongoing theological and professional education, new pastors maintain a vision that enables them to continue growing in their leadership of their congregations. Deborah notes that her enrollment in a DMin program in preaching and worship "helps me keep my sanity in my rural congregation. I can breathe the air of big ideas, maintain my theological integrity, and give something back to my rural congregation."

Bruce often counsels new pastors to take a retreat day each year to reflect on a question around which their whole ministry, both public and private, will pivot: "What can you believe and preach with passion and commitment? What five or ten doctrines can you live or die by at this time of your life?" Then he advises them to take time to write each doctrine down, meditating on the meaning of each one, and then summarize each doctrine in a short, affirmative sentence, such as "I trust God in life and death" or "I believe Jesus calls us to welcome the stranger and outcast" or "God created the universe in the beginning and is still creating today." Faith lives by its heartfelt affirmations. Pastors who are theologically grounded will preach from the heart as well as the mind, from passion as well as intellect. Their words will move persons to take faith seriously in deed as well as in word.

Bruce's recognition of the role of affirmations of faith in sustaining ministry arose from his own hard-won ministerial wisdom. When, after serving for seventeen years as Protestant University Chaplain at Georgetown University, his position was downsized without prior notice, Bruce discovered the power of affirmations to give him a vision of the future and courageously move toward a new life in teaching and ministry. As he explored new vocational possibilities, Bruce was sustained by theological affirmations such as "I can do all things through Christ who strengthens me," "My God will supply all my needs," and "Nothing can separate me from the love of God."[10]

On Becoming a Nonanxious Presence

The Synoptic Gospels tell the story of a great storm at sea. Overwhelmed by the waves and their fear of death, the disciples cry out to Jesus, who had been sleeping peacefully, "Master, Master, we are perishing" (Luke 8:24). According to the story, Jesus awakens and calms the sea with words of peace. As we imagine the story, we visualize that once the disciples realize that Jesus is with them, they begin to feel a sense of peace, even though the waves till rock their skiff. With Jesus with them, they are ultimately safe regardless of the severity of the storm.

Systems thinkers, such as Edwin Friedman and Peter Steinke, assert the importance of remaining a nonanxious presence in congregational leadership.[11] According to systems theory, every congregation and institution becomes anxious in times of uncertainty, change, and conflict. During such times, the anxiety of members is often projected upon those who are perceived to be most vulnerable or powerful within the congregation. At such times, there is often implicit or explicit resistance to the pastor's authority and vision for the church. Resistance, in itself, is not bad, but it is important that a pastor handle it with care.[12] Further, in times of anxiety, institutions often panic and operate according to learned survival mechanisms rather than well-developed plans, imaginative solutions, and generous relatedness. If an anxious system is to experience a sense of dynamic wholeness in times of transition and organizational change, its leadership needs to provide reassurance and guidance. The leadership also needs to be sufficiently centered, grounded, nondefensive, and flexible in its approach to the congregation. Terms such as *reassurance*, *calming*, and *self-differentiation* describe good pastoral leadership in times of transition, uncertainty, and anxiety. Whether it is by meditation, medication, or exercise, a pastor who seeks excellence must learn to minimize and manage her or his own anxiety level.

An encounter between Jesus and his disciples describes the gift of self-differentiation in ministry. After a long day of preaching, teaching, and healing, Jesus got up before sunrise and went to quiet place for prayer. Simon and his companions "hunted" for Jesus and, when they found him, in true triangulating behavior, they chided him with the complaint, "Everyone is searching for you." Centered in God's vision for his life, Jesus responded to the request of the disciples and townsfolk in a rather curious fashion, "Let us go on to the neighboring towns, so that I may proclaim the message there also; for that is what I came out to do" (Mark 1:35-38). Jesus could have acquiesced to their request to become their local chaplain and healer, but Jesus lived by a broader vision, the spreading of God's reign throughout Judea and the world, and that vision guided his decision making, even though it would likely disappoint and anger the townsfolk and disciples.

Healthy ministry involves the fine art of balancing intimacy and care while exploring one's current understanding of God's vision for one's life *and* the congregation's. This means saying no to certain requests in order to say yes to others. As one pastor described her struggle, "I want to help everyone, but there are so many hurting people in this congregation that I need to 'triage' my care for them while respecting my own need for prayer, self-care, and family life. I need to trust that God will find other messengers and healers when I can't show up. I always do my best to call persons immediately and explain to them that I truly care for them, but that I also need to respond to other important needs within the church."

Nearly a decade later, Kate still recalls her dismay in choosing not to make a pastoral call to a church member to whom she had been very attentive during the final stages of cancer. Kate chose to take care of a bad cold. The woman died while Kate was still in bed with a cold. At the time, Kate was able to turn her mixed feelings of grief and regret over to God and regain her health in time to minister effectively to the grieving family. However, she still carries this choice as an example of the burden of self-care and differentiation in ministry.

Self-differentiation provides a crucible within which pastoral care for self and others can flourish. When a pastor has the courage and commitment to live by God's many visions for her life and the congregation, she will faithfully respond from her spiritual center, the place where God whispers in sighs too deep for words, rather than from the crisis of the moment. Operating from an awareness of God's center within his or her own personal center, the healthy minister imaginatively sees the ordinary challenges of ministry in the context of the larger perspective of God's shalom within his or her life and the congregation's. While there is no one path toward experiencing peace amid the storms of ministry, the two of us suggest that pastors in the summertime of ministry endeavor to confront any tendencies toward unhealthy codependence. Required courses on boundary training, which focus on issues of misconduct, are on the tip of the iceberg for many of us who come from enmeshed and dysfunctional families of origin. Preventive and responsive psychotherapy as well as spiritual direction are creative options for many new clergy. Ultimately, healthy pastoral relations in times of stress and challenge arise from the affirmation that ministerial effectiveness comes ultimately by God's grace and not individual achievements.

In the next section, we will focus on pastoral wholeness as the primary foundation for healthy congregational relationships in times of stress and conflict. In the spirit of Psalm 46, a nonanxious presence amid the shaking foundations of congregational life is the gift of trust in God as our refuge and strength and the stillness that enables us to take a deep breath and find perspective so that we can respond creatively rather than react defensively to congregational conflict, triangulation, blame, and resistance.

Wholeness:
Holy Time, Holy Space, Holy Relationships

The foundation of pastoral authority and confidence involves the dynamic interplay of the pastor's basic expertise in the arts of ministry, her or his self-differentiated character, and the vitality of her or his spiritual life. In the Hebraic tradition, pastoral wholeness involves the experience and embodiment of shalom, the healing and wholeness of one's body, mind, spirit, and relationships in light of God's reign of love. Ministry begins with the person and her or his evolving spiritual maturity practiced not only as self-differentiation but also as mind, body, spirit, and relational integration. Accordingly, the quest for personal and relational shalom is a moral and spiritual task. This was the issue for Moses as he tirelessly led the Hebrews through the wilderness. After observing his 24/7 schedule, his father-in-law Jethro observed, "What you are doing is not good. . . . You will surely wear yourself out, both you and those people with you. For the task is too heavy for you, you can't do it alone" (Ex. 18:17-18; see Ex. 18:13-27).

Excellence in ministry in the first years, and throughout one's vocational adventure, arises from the interplay of healthy relatedness, letting go of control, and taking time for sabbath. In the paragraphs that follow, we will present a prescription for pastoral well-being in the transition from seminary to the first congregation, involving holy times and holy relationships. While not exhaustive, this prescription supports pastoral wholeness and centeredness at every stage of ministry. It is no surprise that the spiritual virtues and practices necessary for making a healthy transition from seminary to first congregation build upon the spiritual practices that seminarians ideally discover in the course of a holistic seminary education.

Integrity as Time and Focus

When Bruce was eight years old, he briefly became a neighborhood celebrity by hitting an unexpected home run in a pick-up baseball game. His actual hit barely bounced past first base. But the older boys, trying to trick him, began to shout, "You've still got time, Bruce, you've still got time," as he rounded first base. When they attempted to throw him out at second base, the ball skidded into left field and so Bruce scampered toward third, focusing only on the base path and his destination, as they continued to shout, "You've still got time, Bruce." The throw to third was wild and went into some bushes. The opposing team sadly realized that Bruce did indeed "still have time," when he crossed home plate, leading his team to victory! For the rest of the summer the neighborhood kids greeted Bruce with the nickname "You've still got time," and over the years this statement has become an affirmation of Bruce's contemplative rhythm of academic, administrative, and ministerial work.

Whether one is a contemplative or an activist, "You've still got time" is a helpful affirmation for every pastor. In many ways, the biblical tradition is about the intersection of time and space in God's movement through our lives and through human and planetary history. Throughout the Bible, we see pivotal moments and places—Sinai, the exodus, God's call of Moses, Jesus's healings, Gethsemane—where God's vision for humankind is embodied in the lives of persons and communities. Whether we speak of the grand vision of salvation history or the incarnational images of wisdom literature, God is both omnipresent and omni-active, giving time and space the character of holiness and revelation.

So it is that ministry is ultimately about the mystery of God's time and space, sacred moments and places, where we and our congregants experience and mediate God's touch in the midst of everyday life. Despite the proliferation of literature on time management, every pastor knows that she can't manage time. A Saturday evening, often devoted to polishing off tomorrow's sermon, is interrupted by a call from the hospital emergency room. A knock on the study door alters a pastor's carefully planned morning schedule. A lengthy conversation with a youth leader leads to a life-changing experience, but also a cold supper. While you can't manage your time as a pastor, you can be intentional about how you live the time of your life. The two of us have experienced, however, that it is possible to transform time and to live in alignment with God's *kairos*, in the midst of the fast-moving and constantly vanishing demands of *chronos* time.

Our experience of time is often a matter of subjective interpretation. In his classes on spiritual autobiography, Bruce asks his students to ponder the question, "When does your life story begin? Does it begin with birth or conception? Or, are you connected with your multigenerational family history and the evolution of the universe?" When the biblical tradition proclaims "This is the day that God has made," it roots each day in God's dynamic and graceful creativity from the emergence of the whole universe as well as the calling forth of the Hebraic people into the emergence of the present moment in all its wonder and possibility.

One's interpretation of time, then, is grounded in a vision that is both personal and corporate. Without a vision, both pastor and congregation flounder in the trivial and rush from one task to the other with little or no sense of direction. As we have said earlier, imaginative practices of vision and discernment enable pastors not only to discover God's calling in the midst of time and place but also to provide guidance in prioritizing their vocational and personal responsibilities.

We have found it helpful to realize that in life and ministry we really do only one thing, even though that one thing has many facets. This one thing can be articulated in diverse ways. For Bruce, it is to "do something beautiful for God." For Kate, it is to "love the Creator through loving creation." This overarching vision animates our unique gifts and our vocational and relational responsibilities. Our central calling in life weaves together all of our other callings in such as way that each supports and enhances the others. The integrity of our ability to "equip the saints" for ministries of wholeness and transformation relates to our own ability to nurture a vision for our life and ministry and to follow practices that support God's vision in each of our many vocations.

The quest for a healthy pastoral vision calls a pastor to intentionality, and this intentionality involves articulating a flexible and permeable schedule that reflects her or his vision, values, and priorities in life and ministry. A visionary pastor's schedule of activities also recognizes that care for family and friends is ultimately as important in the practice of ministerial excellence as hospital visitation and sermon preparation. In the dynamic synergy of ministry, excellence in one area requires excellence in all the others. Just try, as a pastor confessed to the two of us, to "write a sermon on healthy relationships after you've argued with your spouse about her perception that you are not being emotionally and physically available" or, as another related, "I'm not ready to lead the midweek healing service until I take time to care for my own body and spirit first."

Both embracing and letting go are essential in this process of scheduling and prioritizing. All decisions, as the philosopher Alfred North Whitehead notes, involve "cutting off" possibilities. If a pastor intends to initiate a contemporary worship service, she must either delegate liturgical and organizational support for another task of ministry or give it up entirely. If a church is embarking on a building campaign and wants the pastor to focus on stewardship and visitation, one of the pastor's first questions should be, "Who will take on the responsibilities I need to let go of in order to meet God's aim at excellence in church leadership at this time?" If a pastor goes on a weeklong Habitat for Humanity project with congregational volunteers, he must remind his congregation that shortly after he returns home he will take several days off for family time and study. Although expectations of pastoral leadership have typically not worked with the concept of overtime or comp time, dedicated pastors still need to educate their congregations about the relationship between study, rest, continuing education, and family time and excellence in ministry.

We suggest that every pastor take three retreats for reflection on a regular basis along with regular spiritual retreats and daily contemplation as ways of discerning and sustaining her or his pastoral vision and maintaining her or his focus amid the daily demands of ministry. The first retreat for reflection involves looking at the big picture of your life at least once a month, imaging the "forest" in its entirety, in order to see your life and ministry as part of something much larger than your day-to-day tasks and responsibilities. This first retreat for reflection involves remembering God's call to ministry and God's evolving call in your life and congregation as the foundation for today's ministerial priorities. It involves attention to the currently growing seeds and expected harvests of ministry over the long haul.

The second retreat for reflection involves regular weekly assessments of the "trees," the details that demand your attention. The dynamic interplay of envisaging the forest and the trees on a regular basis serves as the guide for prioritizing, emphasizing, or eliminating certain pastoral and personal activities. Holding the forest and trees, the broad vision and everyday tasks, in creative contrast helps one discern what is truly important in his or her daily and weekly tasks.

The third regular retreat for reflection focuses on study for the pure joy of it. Over and above the pastor's sermon preparation and devotional reading, a few hours each week committed to theological reflection, movies, poetry, and good literature expands the pastor's perspective on her life and enables her to see God's presence in the small as well as the large responsibilities of ministry. This third retreat is often the most difficult to practice. Theological reflection, "free play," movies, and poetry seem trivial compared to other pastoral responsibilities, but they give zest, vitality, depth, and vision to the rest of a pastor's ministry. One pastor noted that she didn't have time to read until "I discovered how many hours I spent watching TV in the evenings. I still watch my favorite shows but now most nights I spend an hour reading good fiction and theology."

Regular retreats for broad-spectrum visioning, everyday details, and imaginative study will broaden the pastoral imagination and deepen the pastor's sense of vocation, authority, and competence in healthy and life-transforming ways.

The practice of taking pastoral retreats is a reminder that ministry is about space as well as time. Pastoral reflection needs to be rooted in holy spaces in the pastor's daily and weekly routine. As you look at your life of prayer, study, and preparation, where is your holy space? Is it your study at home or at church? Is it a special chair or corner of the den? Is it your garden or the back porch or a local park? Your holy space can even be the local coffee shop or diner where you take a few minutes regularly to gain perspective on the totality of your life and ministry.

The pastor of a rural congregation, Susan's holy place is her home study, also the church study, which she conceptually separates from the rest of the parsonage. She has decorated it with icons and photographs of sacred places and has filled the shelves with her professional library. But, more important, Susan has placed a plaque of the Beatitudes on the inner door of the study. As she goes from the residence to the attached study to make phone calls, meet congregants, or work on her sermon, she pauses to read "Blessed are . . . ." "In that moment of quiet prayer, I find my personal center and consecrate my home study for God's glory. I know that God will inspire everything I do there, if I am truly prayerful."

Time for Everything?

A t-shirt, produced by a Washington, D.C., bookstore, announces, "So many books, so little time." A pastor might well wear a similar t-shirt noting, "So many ministry tasks, so little time." Pastoral ministry is amorphous in nature. With the exception of Sundays and stated meetings and classes, most of the spaces on a pastor's calendar are blank, ready to be filled by the many other moments of pastoral ministry. The flexibility of ministry can either be a source of abundance or scarcity depending on how pastors frame "the time of their lives." One recently ordained pastor notes his great joy in the flexibility of his pastoral schedule: "Every afternoon I can drive home, read a book, and then take a nap with my toddler."

When Kate was a metropolitan D.C. pastor, she avoided driving to the church office until 10 a.m. because of rush-hour traffic. After a leisurely cup of coffee and a walk with Bruce, she often took time to garden, read, or pray before heading to work. When some members complained that she didn't come in early, Kate responded that instead of a forty-five-minute drive at 8:00 a.m., her 10:00 a.m. trip only took fifteen minutes. It was a matter of good stewardship of time. She was using her time wisely to prepare for the challenges of the day ahead and to ground her day in prayer and relatedness. She typically returned home in off hours as well. By avoiding rush hour in her morning and afternoon commutes and pastoral care visits, Kate calculated that she was able to devote an extra one-hundred-fifty hours each year to study and family relationships.

On the other hand, one new pastor found that she couldn't say no to the many possibilities of ministry until one day she set aside an afternoon to examine her calendar. "There were simply no blank spaces on it. I had scheduled meetings with parishioners, committee meetings, and denominational and ecumenical meetings from morning to night. No wonder I had no social life and prepared my sermons on the run." Her life was transformed when she began to add into her calendar regular blocks of time scheduled for prayer and meditation time, study, sermon preparation, and time with friends. As she notes, "I also realized that I had made my appointments entirely at the convenience of others. When I began to make suggestions for appointments that fit into a reasonable schedule of evenings off and Saturdays free, I found that only a few people were inconvenienced, and even then we could find a time that fit both of our needs."

In ministry, we cannot do everything. But successful ministry invites us to follow Eugene Peterson's image of "working the angles"—that is, transforming time through undertaking first the invisible tasks of ministry—prayer, spiritual formation, study—so that our visible ministry will bear great fruit in focus, inspiration, and clarity.[13]

Focus on the Family—and Friends

In the spirit of Genesis 2, the two of us affirm that "It is not good that a pastor be alone." This is as true for urban church pastors as for pastors of rural congregations. The temptation to be a "lone ranger" is immense. There is always more than enough to do each week, and it is easy to let relationships slide, whether with spouses, partners, children, or friends. Time for relational nurture is essential to healthy ministry. Research on pastoral well-being constantly reminds us that we need relationships outside the church in order to have healthy relationships within the church. This takes time—and intentionality.

The amorphous nature of ministerial time and the fact that pastors often work on Saturdays as well as Sundays often places them in a very different time frame than that of their spouses, partners, children, and nonclergy friends. When it's TGIF, or "Miller Time," for a spouse or partner, the pastor may have a wedding rehearsal, need to put the finishing touches on Sunday's sermon, or need to prepare for a church school class. Sunday afternoons often involve youth group, nursing home worship services, and a variety of scheduled or impromptu administrative or pastoral care meetings after church. Too many pastors have felt convicted by the loud protests of their children when they missed another piano recital or soccer game or appear to spend more time with the youth group than their own children!

To be sure, our personal relationships are just as important to the quality of our well-being and the quality of ministry as our professional relationships with congregants. In the dynamically interdependent nature of life, health or disease in one aspect of our lives is contagious—it shapes the quality of every other aspect of our lives. While pastors cannot control the emergencies of ministry, they can plan ahead for times with family, children, and friends, and they should communicate a priority on these relationships to the congregations they serve. To shape one's overall schedule in a way that nurtures his or her deepest relationships is to model healthy relational stewardship. Occasional quality time is no substitute for commitment to set apart quantities of time spent with family and friends. A pastor can't expect holy moments with friends and family to occur if he or she is only around sporadically. One new pastor, who has two daughters in middle school, makes a point to pick them up after school and go for a snack. Another pastor writes in her calendar the dates of special events such as school plays and Little League games in advance and, apart from unexpected serious emergencies, devotes an hour to family time after each event. A recently married pastor plans a date night each week with his wife and limits his evening meetings and study groups to no more than three a week unless it is absolutely necessary. "I need to have a strong relational foundation with my wife if I am to be effective as a pastor. Our happiness together shapes my feelings and creativity in ministry."

Single pastors may need to be even more intentional about taking time for friendships. Often, pastors and congregations alike assume that single pastors, especially women, have "all the time in the world" since they aren't married. The truth is very different. Single pastors need to set time aside for friends outside the church. Finding relationships outside the church requires special intentionality among small town, rural pastors who wish to avoid dual-role relationships. As one rural pastor noted, "When I discovered that I hadn't had a real conversation with someone outside the church for nearly a month, I decided to make some big changes. I called up friends from seminary and arranged for dinners. I made it a point to get to know the other 'under forty' pastors in our conference. I also drive down to the seminary every two weeks to spend lunch with a friend and then the afternoon at the library and bookstore."

Without going into the challenges of dating in the ministry, the two of us recommend that single pastors intentionally find organizations that are outside of the church and their community, especially if they are in rural ministry, in order to widen their relational world as givers and receivers. As Kate says, "Do lots of traveling on your vacations." Charles echoes Kate's sentiment, "I love the church, but life is so much bigger than my congregation. When I get together with colleagues or friends from other professions for dinner or a beer, I get a larger perspective on ministry and feel more confident to face the challenges of my congregation."

During his many years as a university chaplain, Bruce made it a point to come home several afternoons a week. Although he regularly worked at least fifty hours a week, he also regularly planned preparation time and phone calls at home so that he could spend time with our son Matt after school. Between calls and sermon and lecture preparation, they played catch, shot baskets, did homework, and read together. Taking advantage of the flexibility of his schedule, he became a neighborhood surrogate dad to a number of young boys in the neighborhood and was one of the few parents with the time and ability to coach baseball and basketball. One of Bruce's great joys is that he still has relationships with these boys who are now in their late twenties, several of whom participated as groomsmen in his our son Matt's recent wedding that Bruce performed. Kate chose to work three-quarters time so that she could be present for both the ordinary and unique moments of Matt's childhood. Kate felt the sacrifice was well worth it. During our son's childhood, we made a commitment to say no to multiple committee assignments and lecture and workshop engagements in order to parent with constancy and care. Again, our vision and values allowed us to triage our time and focus on what was important. We chose not to say yes to tasks or committees that did not reflect our gifts and passions or support our personal, relational, and family healing and wholeness.

Many new pastors not only make the transition from seminary to their first call but also the transition from seminary to parenting during roughly the same timeframe. Without a doubt, having a child can positively transform your vision of time and ministry. With commitments to family on the horizon, many young pastors choose for the first time to be intentional about relationships and self-care. And this is good! One new mother notes how grateful she is that she can regularly take her baby to church. She works hard but appreciates the flexibility of both space and time as she keeps her child at her side to nurse and care for while she works. She is able to plan her day around naps and feedings as well as make home and hospital visits. While she often goes home in the afternoon to be with her nine-month-old son, she is happy to spend quiet evenings after the baby is in bed preparing her sermons. She notes that having a baby "reminds me of my own needs for rest and re-creation, and the rhythm of my needs is not so different from my child's."

Fathers also learn to balance parenting and ministry. As one father of two young children affirms, "I now filter everything through the lens of my children. While I am often on the go, nearly every day I ask myself if my style of ministry is a good witness to Christ for my children. I want them to know that I love them as much as I love the church."

Each one of these pastors has learned to make the most of his or her time as a result of fully embracing the totality of their lives along with God's call. They do not see themselves solely as pastors or congregational spiritual leaders. While placing ministry and their spiritual growth at the center of their lives, they have developed other interdependent personal "centers," such as family, friends, and holistic spiritual practices. They are learning the concrete meaning of Paul's counsel to "pray without ceasing" (1 Thess. 5:17) as they innovatively mix and blend their core values as pastors, parents, and partners. In the ecology of their lives, today's young ministers in the summertime of their ministries bear witness to the power of daily practices of prayerful intentionality and professional and personal integrity and balance.

Riding without Training Wheels

When our son Matt was in elementary school, Bruce decided to teach him to ride a bicycle. He packed the bike in the trunk of our car and drove to the local middle school where the parking lot was sufficiently isolated and protected for bike riding practice. Every evening for a week, Bruce ran alongside Matt, steadying the bike, pushing a bit, and then letting go. The first few days, Matt rode with training wheels attached to his bike. But, by the fourth day, Matt had picked up enough ability that Bruce could take off the wheels. Eventually, Matt had to ride on his own, wobbling, recovering, and then riding without Bruce's steadying hand. Still, for awhile, Bruce stayed nearby as Matt first circled the parking lot, then the block, and finally was able to ride through the neighborhood without direct supervision.

In many ways, seminary prepares new pastors to "ride" first with training wheels and then on their own. But, despite the best seminary education, new pastors will still need colleagues and mentors to help them stay on a healthy and safe path as they begin the dizzying two-wheel ride of having their own congregation. Like our son Matt, new pastors will wobble and sometimes even fall off. They will occasionally forget their commitments to spirituality, self-care, study, family and friends, and self-differentiation. But, with the companionship of fellow pastors and mentors, they eventually will gain the skills necessary to maintain the spiritual practices, interpersonal skills, and professional habits required for a lifetime of healthy and excellent ministry. As these pastors deepen their commitment to God's presence in their ministries through mutually supportive collegial and familial relationships and to growth through prayer and professional education, they will discover that help is always on the way. In fact, God's help is already here in the midst of the daunting challenges of faithful ministry, mediated through the wisdom of colleagues and mentors and intentional self-care practices.

Supporting Pastoral Excellence for the Summertime of Ministry

As we stated before, it takes a village to nurture the call the ministry. It also takes a village to help new pastors grow creatively and healthfully into their new pastoral identities. As a result of the generosity of the Lilly Endowment, many creative pastoral excellence programs have been initiated by seminaries and judicatories. In the next section, we will describe four pastoral excellence programs, all of which are aimed at supporting the transition from seminary to the first congregational call: (1) Lancaster Theological Seminary's Wholeness in Ministry program, (2) Wesley Theological Seminary's Wesley Fellows, (3) the ecumenical First Parish Project, and (4) the Christian Church (Disciples of Christ) Bethany Fellowships program. These exemplary programs, all of which have been funded by the Lilly Endowment, are superb models for regional and denominational support for pastors in their first season of congregational leadership.

Wholeness in Ministry Program

After nearly a year of consultation and planning, under Bruce's direction, Lancaster Theological Seminary initiated its first Wholeness in Ministry group in January 2005. The Wholeness in Ministry program seeks to support pastors in the transition from seminary to their first congregational call through participation in colleague groups and continuing theological education opportunities that emphasize spiritual formation, wellness practices, and mentoring support.

Avowedly theological in its integration of process-relational theology, systems theory, contemplative spirituality, professional ethics, continuing theological education, and holistic health and self-care, the Wholeness in Ministry program nurtures new pastors through focusing on the lively interplay of mind, body, spirit, and relationships in healthy ministry. Following Paul's affirmation that God will complete the good work God has begun in the lives of ministers, the program uses the imagery of ministry as a marathon rather than a sprint and seeks to encourage habits of wholeness and professional ministry that will sustain pastors throughout their vocational lives. Inspired by Craig Dykstra's concept of the pastoral imagination (see chapter 2), the goal of Wholeness in Ministry is to help pastors practice mindfulness in ministry by asking them to see their daily lives and congregational activities in light of God's vision of wholeness and shalom.

Bruce asks new ministers the same question that he asked first year medical students when he taught at Georgetown University's School of Medicine: "Will you be grateful twenty years from now that you entered this professional field?" Recognizing that well-lived professional lives are a matter of intentionality and choice, as well as good fortune and grace, Bruce also asks new pastors, whether they are twenty-five years old and looking toward a horizon of four decades in ministry or in their midfifties and pondering a professional career of no more than fifteen years, "Will your spouse, partner, children, and closest friends also thank God for your calling into ordained ministry?" How they answer these questions in the daily practice of ministry will greatly depend on their ability to live by a holistic theology of ministry.

The format of the Wholeness in Ministry program centers on participants' involvement in colleague groups of seven to eleven members, each of which meets for three one-day seminars along with two three-day plenary seminars each year over a three-year period. Each colleague group begins with an overnight retreat, co-led by Bruce and an experienced woman minister whose practice of ministry exemplifies a commitment to ongoing theological education, spiritual growth, personal well-being, and congregational leadership and vitality. Each daylong meeting joins prayer, contemplation, and personal sharing of group members' personal and professional lives, with focus on a particular theme that reflects the group's perceived needs and interest. Various groups have focused on themes such as spiritual retreats for pastors, evangelism and mission, time and ministry, excellence and evaluation, nurturing spirituality in the congregation, self-care and balance, money and ministry, dealing with conflict, authority, the liturgical year, appreciative inquiry and personal visioning, pastoral grief, hope in ministry, and congregational stewardship.

Between meetings, Bruce regularly makes pastoral phone calls and occasional visits to participants because he perceives his role as similar to that of a chaplain to the pastors. Participants routinely contact Bruce, Kate, and the other leaders for counsel and mentoring in areas such as congregational visioning, conflict and communication problems with parishioners, illness in the family, personal health issues, maternity leave, holy unions, and continuing theological education. As one participant noted, "My group is a safe place for me to share my doubts and successes without fear of judgment. I can wrestle with an issue, hear the wisdom of colleagues, and know that group members will hold me up in prayer." Another participant affirmed that she could call on "Bruce or one of the co-leaders for counsel when I feel uncertain, over my head, or just need some resources for a congregational program." The confidential nature of these groups enables members to share freely and openly. When it is appropriate, participants receive guidance for ministry, self-care, and family life from other group members.

One example of the benefits of the group's collaborative wisdom occurred in the context of an overnight retreat. In the group meeting, the pastor of a rural congregation shared about an inappropriate unilateral administrative action by one of the congregation's trustees. Although she had been a pastor less than six months, she was convinced that she must confront this pillar of the church immediately and directly, and on her own. After a time of information gathering and prayer, the group's wisdom pointed her in another direction. The group reminded her of the potentially disastrous consequences of a direct and unilateral confrontation, especially since the trustee's family and extended family comprised nearly 20 percent of the congregation's membership. As she listened to the group, this young pastor discerned that she needed to gain broad support from the church board in order to confront this man about his own unilateral decision making. A week later she called Bruce, elated at what had happened. As a result of letting go her idea of an immediate and direct solution to the problem, she discovered that she was not alone in her concern about the trustee's unilateral action. Several other members of the board were disturbed by the trustee's actions and chose to address it as an issue from the board rather than the pastor. The upshot of this new pastor's change in tactics was that she remained on good pastoral terms with the trustee and his family and was able to have a frank and nonargumentative discussion with the trustee on the importance of consultation within the body of Christ. She learned that sometimes good pastoral work requires a pause for reflection rather than an immediate response.

At the heart of the Wholeness in Ministry program is the recognition that healthy, nonanxious, and spiritually grounded pastors contribute directly to the health and well-being of their congregations. There is no substitute for a new pastor's integration of leadership skills with spiritual maturity and personal and relational well-being. Too many well-trained and highly skilled pastors have hurt themselves and their congregations by failing to consider the nurture of their own spiritual lives in effective and transformational ministry. The Wholeness in Ministry program seeks to promote an awareness of this ecology of wholeness in which pastoral well-being is recognized as contributing to healthy congregational transformation.

Ecumenical and inclusive in nature, Wholeness in Ministry embraces newly ordained or called pastors across the all ages and denominational spectrums. Members have ranged from twenty-six to fifty-nine years of age. Behind this multigenerational approach is the belief that although pastors vary in age, they are facing similar developmental challenges as a result of the novelty of their novice experiences in ministry. As one participant noted, "Just because I have gray hair, they think I am experienced in wedding rehearsals and funeral preparation. I felt just as anxious and overwhelmed as my thirty-year-old colleagues when I did my first funeral last week. Although I had a busy week, I was grateful that I came to the new pastors' group and gained wisdom from my younger colleagues that I could use in my funeral preparation."

Bruce has discovered a need for an associate pastors subgroup within the new pastors program. The challenges associate pastors face in multiple-staff congregations vary significantly from those of solo pastors. This group, consisting of several members of different colleague groups, now meets twice yearly to discuss issues of pastoral relationships, boundaries, and spirituality that are unique to associate ministers. An informal group of young mothers and fathers has also emerged as the result of several births among the clergy group families. When controversy raged as a result of the passage of a Marriage Equality resolution at the United Church of Christ's General Synod in 2005, Bruce convened an emergency roundtable, the goal of which was to enable new pastors to respond creatively to the resulting conflict and calls for leaving the denomination or withdrawing funds from within their congregations.

The Lewis Fellows Program

The Lewis Fellows program of Wesley Theological Seminary in Washington, D.C., focuses on the unique concerns and needs of pastors under thirty-five years of age. According to program director Lovett Weems, the percentage of United Methodist pastors under thirty-five has decreased from 15 percent in 1985 to 5 percent in 2007. This same figure would be true for most mainstream Protestant denominations. Weems notes that younger pastors often feel marginalized and isolated in the church as a whole and in their congregations in particular. This reality is heightened by the fact that many young pastors, at the beginning stages of their vocational adventure, are called to small rural and suburban congregations where they find few peers and support systems.

Also funded by the Lilly Endowment, the Lewis Fellows program gathers twenty-four pastors, two peer groups of twelve pastors from a variety of denominations, for five three-day retreats over an eighteen-month period. These retreats involve an integration of theological reflection, spiritual formation, and practical application. According to Weems, the program weaves together "solid theological thinking with the best secular resources on leadership." In the spirit of the early Christian affirmation that "wherever truth is found, God is its source," the Lewis Fellows program is grounded in the belief that "God's wisdom is not limited to theological textbooks" but is found in the insights and expertise of social scientists, systems thinkers, management consultants, and leadership practitioners within and beyond the church. According to Weems, the integration of theology and practice ushers in fruitful ministries that inspire and transform the church.

The Lewis Fellows program is grounded in the recognition that the seminary's "most important constituency is the church." Vital and visionary pastors are essential to vital and visionary congregations. To this end, young pastors are asked to formulate their particular "fruitful leadership project" by identifying some aspect of their ministry that they want to work on in their quest for excellence in pastoral leadership. This enables participants to become more intentional in seeing their day-to-day ministries in light of particular outcomes and goals. According to Weems, this outcome-oriented approach responds to studies that indicate that although parishioners often rate their minister's character and competence highly, they often rate their minister's effectiveness much lower. While success in ministry cannot be measured by the standards of corporate America, effective and transforming congregational ministry is grounded in a clear but open sense of purpose and intentionality that guides everyday and long-term ministerial practices.

Natalya Sharp Cherry is pastor of Christ United Methodist Church in Tower City, Pennsylvania. Bruce had been her professor, university pastor, and mentor in her preparation for seminary, and so we were delighted that Natalya was an early participant in the Lewis Fellows program. As she reflects on her experience as a Lewis Fellow, Natalya notes that "one of the greatest problems new pastors face is loneliness. In the Lewis Fellows program, I had the opportunity to share with peers in ministry." A unique aspect of the Lewis Fellows is its focus on leadership development. According to Natalya, "We had the opportunity to experience different forms of pastoral leadership assessments as a way of discerning our own particular leadership style. We were also encouraged to formulate a leadership plan for ourselves and our congregation."

First Parish Project

When Mark graduated from seminary, he was delighted that his first call was to a thriving rural congregation. In contrast to the aging congregations of the metropolitan area that he had experienced growing up and in college, his rural congregation of one hundred Sunday worshipers had a solid contingency of young families, persons in midlife, and senior adults. But several months into his ministry, Mark discovered that although the congregation continued to grow and was quite excited about having a young pastor with a spouse and two young children, he and his wife were beginning to feel isolated and lonely in ministry. His nearest professional colleagues were pastors in their late fifties who served conservative and fundamentalist churches and with whom he had virtually nothing in common. He felt that they judged him not only because of his youth but also because of his theological openness. His denomination's local ministerium was dominated by male pastors in midlife or on the verge of retirement. Although the congregation was thriving, virtually no one stopped by his parsonage study except to drop off their children for confirmation class. Mark and his wife both felt isolated by their profession, age, and location. Both of them needed peers who spoke their own language and could help them face the challenges of ministry in rural America.

Mark represents the type of pastor whose first experience in ministry inspired the First Parish Project of the Hinton Rural Life Center in Hayesville, North Carolina. Although the First Parish Project focuses on pastors whose congregations typically number under a hundred worshipers each Sunday, it responds to challenges young pastors face as they make the transition not only from seminary to their first congregational call, but also from mid- to large-sized suburban and urban congregations to rural or declining urban settings.[14]

Also funded by the Lilly Endowment, the First Parish Project looks for pastors who "understand that they need to develop healthy spiritual practices as well as habits of self-care, and for men and women who know that they need assistance in developing congregational systems such as planning and visioning."[15] Clay Smith, who directs the program, notes the challenges of young pastors in addressing the needs of multigenerational congregations: "Americans are very attuned to age cohorts. And yet, when young pastors are in their first assignment, they are asked to minister to people who range in age from five to ninety-five, and the bulk of the persons who are active in congregations are most likely twenty to thirty years older than the young pastor. This is something very real that they are not prepared for when they begin their ministry. One of the goals of this program is to connect these young ministers with people their own age who are having shared cultural experiences."

Groups of approximately twenty-four pastors meet Monday to Friday six times during an eighteen-month period at the Hinton Center for worship, prayer, personal reflection, and study, rotating between small- and large-group programs. The rural environment and geographical isolation of the Hinton Center provides a retreat-like atmosphere that promotes prayer and personal reflection. Further, the weeklong retreat enables pastors to rest and re-create; they "allow themselves to receive hospitality, rather than provide it, for a few days," according to Clay Smith. Between retreats, participants communicate in a weekly online chat room. Young pastors are nurtured intellectually, practically, spiritually, and relationally so that they can minister to their small congregations in healthy and competent ways.

According to Lance Mullins, a graduate of Columbia Theological Seminary, Decatur, Georgia, and pastor of New Covenant Metropolitan Community Church in Laurel, Maryland, "What was central to my experience and what sustained me in congregational ministry was a community of colleagues. While making friends in seminary was easy, finding friendships among colleagues once you are in the parish is extremely difficult." The First Parish

Project enabled Lance to find an ecumenical community of peers with whom he could share the joys and challenges of ministry and receive encouragement and counsel.

The Bethany Fellowships

The Bethany Fellowships represents a denominational attempt to nurture young pastors. Another project funded by the Lilly Endowment, the Bethany Fellowships is a program aimed at nurturing excellence in ministry among younger pastors in the Christian Church (Disciples of Christ) as they make the transition from seminary to congregational ministry. Virtually all the participants are in their first career and range from twenty-four to thirty-five years of age. The focus of the Bethany Fellowships is on individual mentoring, collegial accountability, best practices in ministry, and spiritual formation. Similar to the Wholeness in Ministry program sponsored by Lancaster Theological Seminary, Bethany Fellows learn that "the call to ministry is not just about what we do, but is also, even primarily, about who we are." Participants also receive regular contacts from program mentors who, like the colleague group leaders in the Wholeness in Ministry program, join success in ministry with a commitment to their own spiritual growth.[16]

Twice yearly, Bethany Fellows gather for a five-day retreat that integrates prayer, collegial support, best practices in ministry, and quiet contemplation. According to program director Don Schutt, these retreats provide "a liminal space in which participants can learn best practices in ministry from experienced pastors and deepen their spiritual lives." At the heart of each retreat is a period of silence that extends from Tuesday evening to Thursday morning. Far from phone calls and the demands of programs and parishioners, young pastors have an opportunity to contemplate their life and ministry in the interplay of silence and community. They often receive new insights about their lives and ministries. One participant in the Bethany Fellowships noted that it was during one time of extended silence that she "really learned to pray."

The goal of this four-year collegial program is, according to Don Schutt, to form "a generation of leaders," who will spend thirty to forty years in ministry, who will join the journey inward and the journey outward in a way that integrates personal and professional transformation with the transformation of congregational life.

Laura Jean Torgerson is a Disciples of Christ minister who serves as the pastor of youth and family life at Cleveland Park Congregational United Church of Christ in Washington, D.C. Laura Jean's experience in the Bethany Fellowships joined solitude and community. On the one hand, Laura Jean notes that the encounter with other young Disciples of Christ pastors of her own age group "filled me with hope about the future of the church and my denomination. It was inspiring to see so many great people who were doing great things. That others were doing great things reminded me I could do great things as well." On the other hand, prior to coming to her first Bethany Fellowships retreat, Laura Jean confesses that "two hours was the most time I spent in silence. But, at the retreat, I spent thirty-six hours in silent prayer and meditation, and had my first experience of spiritual direction." According to Laura Jean, the Bethany Fellowships "sustains us in ministry and gives us the time and space to pay attention to our spiritual needs."[17]

Spiritual Practices for the Summertime of Ministry

The following activities offer help for facing challenges and growing in integrity as you adventure through ministry's summertime.

The Encircling

From the Celtic tradition comes a prayer form called "the encircling." Whenever Celtic adventurers began their journeys, whether across the moors or the sea or simply to market, they often practiced the *caim,* or encircling, as a reminder that they were in God's protective care. With their index finger facing outward, they rotated themselves in clockwise direction, inscribing a circle around themselves. As new ministers encounter the challenges of ministry for the first time, they often feel alone and unprotected. When you anticipate a stress-producing situation, take time to physically or mentally draw a circle of God's protection around you and say a prayer asking God to remind you of God's ever-present care and protection. Our experience is that God gives the guidance and support a person needs to flourish in every situation. The task is simply to claim it.

A Relational Check

Every so often it is important to sit back and take stock of our lives. In certain spiritual communities, this mindfulness is described as an examination of conscience. For busy pastors, reflecting mindfully on the health of their relational lives is essential.

The two of us find it helpful to take a few minutes for quiet meditation, breathing deeply and gently at first. Allow yourself to come to a place of rest and comfort of mind, body, and spirit as you reflect on the quality of your relational life. You may choose to ponder and journal about questions such as:

- How much time do I spend with loved ones (spouse, partner, child/children, good friends)?
- How do I characterize that time? What is the quality of my emotional presence? What is the quality of my listening and sharing? Am I distracted by the tasks of ministry? What do I feel as I listen and share with loved ones?
- What activities are currently involved in my relational life—eating, sports and recreation, walking, physical touch and intimacy, and so forth? What activities might be missing that would be helpful to initiate for the sake of body, mind, spirit, wellness?

- In what ways do I experience God in my closest relationships? How might I feel God's presence more intimately in my relationships?

After a time of quiet reflection, prayerfully invite God to inspire you with insights regarding ways you might bring greater joy and presence to your closest relationships.

Covenant of Spiritual Transformation for Summertime in Ministry

Issues of intellectual, spiritual, and relational integrity are significant among the many challenges in the transition from seminary to first congregational call. You may choose to make a covenant of spiritual transformation along the lines of the following affirmations or choose your own covenantal adventure.

- I covenant to spend time in study and share my insights in ways that deepen my congregation's spiritual life and theological reflection.
- I covenant to seek moments of silence each day, and when I begin to feel busy or anxious, to stop for a moment and take a few deep and prayerful breaths to bring myself back to God's center in my life.
- I covenant to spend holy, loving, and playful time with my loved ones on a regular basis.

๔ 4 ๖

Autumn in Ministry

Endurance and Transformation

In central Pennsylvania where we live, autumn is a glorious season. The two of us delight in sitting on our back porch as the days grow shorter and cooler, bathing our eyes in the changing colors of the forest behind our home. We rejoice in walking on blustery days, surrounded by a shower of falling leaves. On weekends we take "color tours" throughout the countryside and often stop at roadside markets to gather the fruits of the fall harvest—squash, pumpkins, apples, and cider.

Fall is a time of bright red, yellow, and orange; shorter days; transformation; and letting go. Winter is on the horizon and the changing colors forecast cold days and bare trees. Although both of us have experienced the cycle from summer to fall and the yearly ritual of bright colors and falling leaves for more than fifty years, we seek to approach the season with an open spirit and a beginner's mind because each fall brings something new to the environment and our lives. As the two of us move toward our own personal autumns in ministry and academic life, the spirit of autumn calls us to rejoice in the harvest of a good life, the fruitfulness of faithful ministry, the impact we have made on others, and the need to embrace creativity and change as the prelude to the next adventure.

Bursting Forth without Burning Out

One of our favorite stories from the Christian spiritual tradition tells of a North African monk who visits his spiritual director in search of counsel for the next steps of his faith journey. As the two spiritual companions share their spiritual journeys, Abbot Lot reveals to Abbot Joseph his quest for more vital spiritual experience, "I keep my little rule, and my little fast; my prayer, meditation, and contemplative silence; and according as I am able I strive to cleanse my heart of thoughts: now what more should I do?" His companion stood up, raised his hands to heaven, and his fingers shot forth "ten lamps of fire" as he replied, "why not become totally changed into fire!"[1]

Bidden or unbidden, fall bursts forth in fire, whether in the cornfields or the life of a committed pastor, reaching the prime of her or his professional life. This bursting forth reflects not only the natural flow of life but also the willingness of pastors to embrace the wisdom of aging and the realities of change and novelty. Ministry, like the seasons, is a cyclical profession. Pastors live their professional lives from Sunday to Sunday, from stewardship campaign to stewardship campaign, from rally day to rally day, from board meeting to board meeting, and from Advent to Advent. The repetitive acts of ministry can be a source of creativity or boredom. Like thorns that infest a garden, they can, year after year, choke the spiritual life that bursts forth with our initial call to ministry and first congregation, or they can be like the fertile soil from which new and colorful ministerial practices emerge.

With each new Sunday's passing, most pastors catch their breath and begin to turn their attention toward next Sunday's sermon. In the course of a thirty-year ministry, a pastor cycles through the three-year lectionary ten times, not to mention thirty Advents, Lents, Holy Weeks, and Easters. As one pastor notes, "In my first years everything was fresh. I saw everything with new eyes. My first Easter and Christmas were overwhelming. I encountered many lectionary readings as if I'd never seen them before. I was in love with the lectionary texts, and waited expectantly for each new insight the Spirit would give me. Then, I hit a lull. It all seemed old and familiar. I had trouble finding anything new, and I recycled parts of sermons from the past liturgical cycle. Sometimes all I saw were words with no spirit behind them. But, now, following a continuing education course at the seminary on preaching the Gospel of Matthew, everything is new again. I never knew the many dimensions of the Gospel. I can't wait for Monday morning to start all over again. It's like I'm seeing the Bible again for the first time!"

Another pastor, now midway into her second decade of ministry, confessed, "Each year I struggle to say something new at Christmas and Easter. I no longer understand these stories literally as I once did. But still I want to enter Christmas with the eyes of child and Easter as if I'd just lived through Good Friday and Holy Saturday. I want to be surprised again. But I realize that I need to be transformed if the stories are to take on new life for myself and the congregation."

Sometimes clergy experiencing a certain repetitive dullness in their midlife careers need to be jolted into newness. Lutheran pastor Heidi Neumark experienced the unexpected fall of a tree as a divine call to renew her ministry, despite several strong years in her Bronx parish. "One day the big tree in front of the church fell over and crashed onto my van, almost totaling it. A slight breeze toppled it. To everyone's surprise, the tree turned out to be completely rotten inside. The outside looked fine and was still putting out leaves."[2] Neumark recognized that she, like the fallen tree, had been slowly suffocating in body and spirit, despite her deep commitment to seeking justice and providing pastoral care in her ministry in one of the most challenging neighborhoods of the Bronx. As she listened to her body-mind-spirit life signals, she noticed that she was short of breath, spiritually shriveling, and impatient with those she loved most. Neumark asked herself, "Was this the beginning of burnout? It might have been, but it wasn't. Writing kept me from going over the edge again. Writing became a door for contemplation and a channel for grief."[3] Ironically, *Transfiguration*, the name of the church Neumark served, held the clue to her spiritual and personal transformation. In listening to her life, Neumark heard the call of reflection and writing as her own antidote to the grief, repetition, and struggle that builds up within a pastor after many years in congregational ministry. Instead of burning out and toppling like the neighborhood tree, Neumark was transfigured by a mystical transformation similar to that which author Annie Dillard calls "the tree with lights," the unexpected gift of a new sense of beauty and wonder in the everyday tasks of ministry. What seemed like repetition was transformed into holy ground for herself and her congregation.

Rabbi Abraham Joshua Heschel describes radical amazement as one of the primary religious virtues. At midcareer in ministry, pastors need to experience the polar virtues of endurance and transformation as they confront familiar tasks with new eyes. For seventeen years, Bruce served as the Protestant chaplain at Georgetown University. Every August brought a new crop of first-year students, many of whom knocked on his study doors in September with the same issues that their predecessors had brought the year before—loneliness, homesickness, and spiritual uncertainty. After several years Bruce could almost anticipate their questions and struggles and if they paused for even a moment, he was tempted to complete their sentences. Challenged by the reality of repetition, Bruce, like Heidi Neumark, knew that he had to be spiritually transformed in order to respond creatively and sensitively to the needs of his university flock. After all, the stories he had heard year after year were new to the storytellers. He realized that repetition could be a call to spiritual depth rather than boredom. Within the stories he heard, Bruce chose to discover a ritual and a liturgy, a call and response, that enabled him to experience each student as if he or she were his first and only parishioner. Bruce found his key to freshness in pastoral care through two simple practices—first, he said a brief silent prayer before he answered his ringing phone or opened his study door, and, second, whenever he began to feel weary of the repetition, he would step out of his study for a short walk around campus. He always returned renewed and able once again to encounter each story as a unique testimony to a student's quest for God's presence in her or his life.

Ministry and liturgy are grounded in repetitive ritual. While ritual can lead to lifeless routine, life-supporting rituals such as meditation and communion deepen our faith and integrate conscious and unconscious experience. Our bodies as well as our spirits are transformed by the practices and rituals of our lives, and it is our job to renew our practices, especially in midcareer in ministry. When one pastor, Susan, takes her first deep breath as she prepares for her daily practice of yoga, she is immediately flooded by a sense of peace that embraces her mind, body, and spirit, despite the challenges that she knows the day will bring. Another pastor feels a sense of centeredness in worship as he closes his eyes a moment before reciting Psalm 19:14: "Let the words of my mouth and the meditation of my heart, be acceptable to you, O LORD, my rock and my redeemer," as he prepares to begin each Sunday's sermon. Kate has learned to experience greater peace and insight in ministry through her participation in the Oasis Ministries program for spiritual leaders and regularly practicing breath prayers, as taught by Thich Nhat Hanh.[4]

Rituals shape the way we experience the world. Healthy spiritual practices are rituals that join what physician Herbert Benson calls the "relaxation response," a sense of physical and spiritual "remembered wellness," with Paul's call to ceaseless growth and creative transformation: "Be not conformed to this world, but be transformed by the renewing of your minds" (Rom. 12:2).[5] In the repetition of ministerial acts year after year, many pastors begin to experience "brown out," but they can avoid burnout if they seek renewal though a lively balance of order and novelty, stability and change, and endurance and transformation, which are necessary to healthy and effective ministry in midcareer. This is a matter of grace and gift, but it is also a commitment to transformational practices amid the routine events of ministry.

Barbara Brown Taylor's book *Leaving Church* describes what happens when a pastor forgets the importance of deep intentionality in her quest for ministerial excellence and congregational growth. In her attempt to be a pastor to everyone, Taylor forgot that the primary embodiment of ministry is the pastor her- or himself. She had forgotten that in order to share God's grace in healing and effective ways over the long haul, pastors need to awaken to that same healing and restoring grace within their own lives.

Listen to Barbara Brown Taylor's words of confession. After leaving a thriving downtown church where she served as associate rector to take a position in the gentle Georgia countryside, she discovered that she had brought with her the same behaviors and attitudes that nearly destroyed her in her fast-paced urban parish. In her own words, she was "so busy caring for the household of God that I neglected the One who called me there. . . . Feeding others was my food. As long as I fed them, I did not feel my own hunger pangs."[6] She had forgotten her soul in her commitment to her role as parish priest. Always on duty and at the beck and call of her parish, she succumbed to "tiresome perfectionism, need for approval, and the judgment of other pastors."[7] She soon found herself the victim of compassion fatigue, going through the motions of good ministry but never truly really there for herself, her parishioners, or her husband. Sadly, because she could not change her attitudes and behaviors, Taylor's only salvation was to leave the pastoral ministry entirely.

Our word of grace to you is that you can be transformed. You don't have to leave congregational ministry to experience wholeness of mind, body, and spirit. You can experience vital and transforming ministry in every season of life. The good news of the gospel is that grace abounds and that pastors can change their habits, lifestyle, and approach to ministry! Pastors can become healed healers, rather than burnt-out functionaries.

But pastors need to confront creatively the challenges of midlife in ministry in order to turn the dying fires into beautiful autumn landscapes. While the list is not exhaustive, the two of us believe that experiencing transformation and developing staying power in the autumn of ministry involves the following:

- Confronting grief and loss in ministry
- Cultivating novelty in responding to the everyday tasks of ministry

- Letting go of perfectionism and indispensability
- Taking responsibility for your own health and well-being
- Finding harvest in midlife
- Rediscovering your first love in ministry

Healing the Grieving Pastor

Take a moment to ponder the necessary and unavoidable losses that accompany the process of aging in the vocation of congregational minister. What losses have you experienced as a pastor or a pastor's spouse or partner? How did you respond to these losses? In what ways did you find healing and wholeness amid transition? Where are you able to be creative?

In the course of a long-term ministry, loss and grief are unavoidable precisely because change is unavoidable. Hear what author Judith Viorst might describe as the "necessary losses" in a long-term ministry.[8]

Moving

Most pastors move several times in the course of their careers. Moving to a new congregation often involves uprooting their families, moving to a new home, and letting go of close relationships in their former churches. While appropriate boundaries between pastors and former parishioners are essential, we regret that most boundary training is framed from a dualistic, pathology-oriented Newtonian framework that neglects to deal with the pain felt by the pastor and her or his family as they move from pastorate to pastorate. The pain of leaving a congregation is often increased by ministerial successors and judicatory officials who are overly cautious at boundary drawing with departing pastors. Ministerial departures, unlike many other professional leave takings, involve a clear and immediate suspension of long-term relationships. However, we have found it helpful, on occasion, to consult with our predecessors about various congregational patterns of dealing with conflict and to update them about serious health issues or deaths among congregants with whom they were personally close.

Death

While pastors are called to be professional in dealing with death, we clergy also mourn the death of parishioners, especially those with whom we have forged intimate and healthy pastoral relationships. Often pastors must hide their tears and discharge their grief elsewhere in order to support the grief of family members and the church community. At times, there is no place for a pastor to grieve safely.

Loss of Membership

Many pastors mourn the fact that, despite their best efforts, their congregations and denominations are losing members. Even the best evangelism and new member programs may fail to revitalize an aging congregation. As one pastor notes, "It breaks my heart each week to see so many empty pews in what was a vital congregation when I came a decade ago. Although I rationally know that demographic changes in the neighborhood are a major factor, I still feel like a failure each Sunday. But I have to put on a happy face and cheer them up because they're grieving too."

Many pastors grieve families who leave as a result of the culture wars in the church or because of their desire to have different or more "uplifting" worship. "Sometimes I'm glad when I see families leave the church, especially when I know that we are not right church for them. But I will miss them. And I feel like we've let them down by not being open enough to their conservatism or flexible enough in our worship style," confesses one pastor.

Personal Limitations

In midlife, a person becomes all too aware of roads not taken, the impact of her or his decisions, and her or his own aging process. One pastor notes, "I've always been healthy, but now I wake up feeling aches and pains after a good day of gardening or golf." Another confesses, "I wonder what would have happened if I'd accepted that suburban pastorate. Now that I'm fifty-seven and I think that I'll always be a country pastor, I wonder what it would be like to be near the symphony, a good movie theater, and a congregation comprised of college graduates. I guess I'll never know."

Whether in ministry or medicine, the cost of not facing professional grief can be disastrous, leading to substance abuse, compassion fatigue, and burnout. When grief is not addressed, it saps our vitality and robs us of zest for life. It also may surface in unexpected anger and alienation or withdrawal from persons who love us.

Clearly, change is essential to a good life that reflects God's own ever-changing and ever-faithful love. But change is always difficult. Studies on the impact of grief note that even positive changes in a person's life, such as finding the congregation of one's dreams, can be stress and grief producing. In every season of life, moving ahead means letting go, whether it's the first day of college, graduation from seminary, one's first congregation, or being called to lead a healthy, strong multiple-staff congregation at midlife. The unavoidable pain of letting go of the past in order to embrace the present and future calls us as pastors, and people, to self-examination and to finding adequate support among trusted friends and mentors. Friends on the journey help us gain perspective as they listen to our stories and feelings and help us work through the various forms of grief in the autumn of our ministries.

Midcareer grief calls pastors to reflect on their own personal theology and philosophy of life and to assess its adequacy for the long haul—how a person's hopes and dreams relate to her or his aging and cumulative losses. To recognize that change is inevitable and that limitation is necessary in a well-lived life is the first step to finding new possibilities for spiritual transformation. Limitation is part of life, but the decisions we make and the attitudes we have toward them can be the soil from which new life springs. Within every situation, there lie hidden seeds of new life. Pastoral imagination opens one's eyes to surprising possibilities for both personal growth and achieving pastoral excellence within ordinary congregational settings.

It is important, however, to note that there is a clear difference between the autumnal experiences of "first career" pastors (who have known no other career in the course of their lifetime) and the increasingly common "second career" pastors, who may be experiencing physical aging but whose zeal for ministry is fresh and new. While one would expect that second-career pastors could learn much from well-seasoned first-career, lifelong pastors and their midlife wisdom, the two of us have also seen that their experience in ministry is so vastly different that we recommend dividing them into separate colleague groups, whenever possible.

Autumnal grief calls for expression in creative words, actions, and tears. While the expression of grief varies from person to person, the two of us believe that the wisdom of the Psalms reminds pastors that they can share their pain with God in the context of a trusting community, whether it is a colleague group, therapist, spiritual director, or trusted friend. Contrary to one's greatest fears, a person's tears are a wellspring within which the seeds of ministry grow. As Granger Westberg once noted, grief is good when one creatively embraces and processes it.[9] When pastors experience their own ongoing healing of grief, they can pastor others more faithfully.

Cultivating Novelty in Ministry

A Buddhist saying notes that "before enlightenment I chopped wood and carried water, and after enlightenment, I chopped wood and carried water!" This applies to ministerial transformation as well. The philosopher Alfred North Whitehead asserted that higher organisms flourish because they originate novelty to match the novelty of the environment.[10]

Studies as well as the anecdotal experiences of pastors suggest that ministerial happiness is related to ongoing continuing education. Another way to describe the practice of continuing ministerial education is the commitment to doing old things in new ways and seeing the ordinary from a new perspective. If the practical meaning of the theological term *divine omnipresence* is that God is present in every moment and every task, always doing a new thing, then it follows that we need the "mundanity of creativity" to complement our commitment to the "mundanity of excellence." Creative and novel ministerial responses to regular as well as unexpected aspects of ministry are not accidental but arise from an ongoing commitment to grow in one's pastoral imagination as well as one's theological and spiritual stature.

When she accepted the call to be senior pastor of a midsized suburban congregation, Susan could have deferred her dream of pursuing a DMin at Lancaster Theological Seminary. Although on some busy days she questions the wisdom of her decision, she knows that the benefits of the collegiality and the exposure to new ideas she experiences in the DMin program enliven her soul and her sermons. Wishing to share her own personal growth with her congregation, Susan has also initiated classes in yoga and study groups in progressive Christianity in her rather traditional congregation. She has also initiated a congregational study process, using Roy Oswald's *Discerning Your Congregation's Future*.[11] She is willing to take risks born of her process of self-differentiation and exploration. While she respects the traditions of her congregation, she knows that congregational vitality in the future depends on a pastor and a congregation that embrace new ways of experiencing the past as they anticipate the future.

Dean, a Disciples pastor in the mid-Atlantic, articulates his growing edge as being about discovering the balance between the routine and the novel. Dean affirms that "it's all about balance. Ministry has many facets. Depending on your personality, certain things can give you energy, other things can sap your energy. While too much administration drains me, my focus on what gives me energy—worship and outreach—brings vitality to my administrative work. When I see the spirit moving in our church in new ways, every aspect of my ministry comes alive. Variety enlivens my ministry." Recently, Dean became the leader of his community's rebuilding after a natural disaster. By his own admission, while he did a creative job in marshaling the resources of his small community, he eventually found himself personally and pastorally overwhelmed by the details as well as the conflicts involved in rebuilding the community. Although he at first resisted his wife's counsel, he eventually decided to seek the counsel of a therapist who specializes in working with pastors. "I needed new perspective on my work. I was burning the candle at both ends without any replenishment. I needed someone to reflect back to me what I was saying and to alert me about healthy paths I might take." Dean notes that most caregivers resist seeking care for themselves. In pursuing personal counseling, Dean sought novelty—a new perspective on his work—to respond creatively to the repetitive demands of his ministry. "We [pastors] believe," Dean confesses, "that we can solve our problems on our own. I believed that my calling was to take care of others and not myself. I needed permission to take time out for self-care." Today, Dean is living out of the abundance he finds as he combines everyday tasks with new adventures of psychological growth and personal exploration. Now, with fifteen years of ministry behind him, he is looking forward to what's next in his ministry.

David, a United Methodist pastor from Alabama, asserted "I love change," when Bruce asked him about his own approach to ministry. "I enjoy doing new things and being a change agent, although some days I wish for a little boredom in my ministry." David entered the DMin track in leadership at Wesley Theological Seminary as a way of being more intentional about his role in congregational transformation. As a seminary student once again, he is discovering new and helpful ways to support his congregation's need for transformation. David is also discovering novelty in ministry as a result of the birth of his first child. Prone to being a workaholic, David has discovered vitality through a commitment to home and family that now structures his ministry in healthful ways. "When I open the door and my eighteen-month-old son cries 'Da, Da,' I know that home is as important as church for my spiritual growth and professional excellence," he says. For David, the biggest change has been to let go of being involved in every event and every meeting in his thousand-member congregation. "That's a big challenge for me, letting go of control, but I know God wants me to be a good parent, too, and get out of the way so my parishioners take on their role as church leaders." Fortunately, David has a child and spouse who constantly remind him that caring for his family is a calling of equal value to his ministry.

Perhaps one of the most challenging aspects of midlife in ministry is a pastor's unexpected discovery that he or she is now a member of "the sandwich generation." As one pastor relates, "I am working hard to find balance between responding to my aging parents, my college-age children, and the needs of my congregation. For a while I felt guilty all the time. There were just too many demands and not enough time. I was verging on compassion fatigue. I experienced a new sense of freedom when my conference pastor reminded me that my care for my family was also my ministry."

A respected spiritual guide also reminded her that her ability to take care of others depended on her own spiritual and physical well-being. "I used to say yes to everything and find myself on the run from morning to night. The demands of my aging parents forced me to reevaluate my approach to ministry as well as my own self-care. Now, I block out an hour each day simply to take care of myself—to read a good book, work in the garden, pray, or go on a walk with my husband. Since I began to be intentional about self-care, I've discovered, much to my amazement, that I have more energy and time for both my family and my ministry." She has been intentional in embracing new ways of balancing pastoral ministry, spiritual formation, and care for her family. She notes that "although the church now gets less of me in terms of hours, it now gets more of me as a healthy pastoral leader and compassionate preacher. My healthy commitment to balancing care for my parents and children with care for myself and my marriage has enabled me to respond more sensitively to the pastoral needs of my congregation."

Be not conformed to this world of pastoral expectations, but be transformed by the renewing of your mind and attitudes toward yourself, your ministry, and your loved ones. The prophetic imagination noted by Walter Brueggemann involves exploring an alternative reality to our present lifestyle and values.[12] The pastors described above looked at the challenges of their ministries and saw them as a creative opportunity rather than a crisis of aging and responsibility. They chose to awaken to God's call for creative transformation and initiated novelty—a DMin program and congregational visioning; a therapeutic relationship; a change in lifestyle and commitments to family and self-care—that enabled them to grow professionally as well as personally. Despite the ongoing demands that they face in their quest for excellence in ministry, these and many other pastors in the autumn of their ministries delight in their work precisely because they have taken the time to change their attitudes and behaviors.

Letting Go of Perfectionism

According to a Jewish legend, Rabbi Zusya once stated, "In the world to come, I shall not be asked, 'Why were you not Moses?' Instead, I will be asked, 'Why were you not Zusya?'" Every season of life calls us to our own unique vocation for this time and place. It need not be perfect, only authentic, in order to respond to God's calling in our lives.

Self-awareness is at the heart of healthy and effective ministry in midlife. Pastors who take the time to reflect upon their lives and ministry recognize the interplay of limitation and possibility that yields a well-lived professional life. The dynamic wisdom of aging tells us that the choices we make and the roads we travel open us to surprising adventures, but they also cut us off from an array of possibilities. While pastors are called to do greater things for God than we can even imagine, ministerial self-awareness is guided by the wisdom of graceful imperfection. In the concrete world of personal decision-making and congregational life, we can never do it all, nor should we even attempt to be the perfect, all-around pastoral caregiver, preacher, teacher, change agent, and spiritual guide.

Healthy and mature pastors have discovered their personal and professional gifts and limitations and hold themselves accountable to them as they seek to mediate God's grace to their particular congregations. In a world that identifies professional success with productivity and numerical growth of the sort boasted by corporate America, one's humble, accountable quest for pastoral excellence is always informed and consoled by recognition of the failures and misadventures of the heroes and heroines of the biblical story. In previous chapters we have considered Jonah's defiance and Esther's reticence; we also recall Peter's vacillating faith, Paul's conflicts with other Christian leaders, and the disciples' cowardice in crisis. Recognizing the fallibility of humankind and the inherent limitations of life, Mother Teresa reminds us that our calling as followers of Jesus is not to be successful by the world's standards, but to be faithful to the God who calls us to partnership in healing the world.

From the perspective of the pursuit of ministerial excellence and wholeness, we have found that perfectionism in ministry is one of the greatest enemies of pastoral excellence. Destined to see themselves as failures when judged by the elusive horizon of perfection, many pastors constantly seek to prove their worth by attending one more meeting, working another hour to write the perfect sermon, and making another pastoral call while their own family waits impatiently to leave for a holiday. Others compromise their integrity by "borrowing" what they believe to be better-crafted sermons from the Internet or other clergy. Although they preach the grace of God to their congregations, many pastors are anything but graceful when it comes to their own personal lives.

The wisdom of graceful imperfection is grounded in the pastor's humble recognition that grace abounds for her- or himself as well as for the congregation. Bruce recalls the ironic words of his Jesuit spiritual guide who challenged Bruce's ongoing quest for the perfect spiritual practice—"If it's worth doing, it's worth doing poorly!" At that moment, Bruce realized that he didn't need to add another spiritual practice to his current repertoire of contemplative techniques in order to experience spiritual enlightenment; his calling was simply to be faithful in practicing the ones that best complemented his personality and schedule.

While pastors in every season are called to excellence in ministry, pastors are equally challenged to consider the lilies of the field and the birds of the air, and how they neither toil nor spin (Matt. 6:28). The greater things that pastors are called to embody in their ministries are always concrete and contextual, limited by past decisions and congregational systems but also inspired by God's open future.

For Heidi Neumark, the struggle to experience the wisdom of graceful imperfection meant accepting God's call into the little things of ministry rather than the grand achievements of pastoral leadership. "It seems that every time I open a church magazine, I am instructed to raise my expectations, higher and higher. But over the years I have lowered my expectations, and it has made me freer and happier. I am more accepting of my limitations and more aware of the grace of God working when I cannot."[13]

An American Baptist pastor, Barbara, tells of her struggle to recover from pastoral indispensability. "I used to think that my worth as a pastor was based on my always being there for my parishioners. I had to go to every congregational committee meeting and denominational gathering. I had to visit every shut-in on a regular basis and sit at every hospital bedside. I felt they couldn't get along without me in times of crisis and decision making. But, perhaps, I was worried that they *could* get along without me, and I didn't want them to get a chance to find out!" Although she was recognized as an excellent pastor, Barbara's own personal distress challenged her to realize that she had been "too good" a pastor for her own and her congregation's well-being. "My goal today is to be a 'good enough' pastor, one who is caring and compassionate, but who also gives the congregation room to grow by faithful trial and error." As she has grown and matured in ministry, Barbara has realized that her "good enough" ministry, characterized by regular days off, quarterly retreats, and time with her family, has opened the door to greater lay leadership in her congregation in addition to her own increased well-being.

Barbara has learned the art of dispensability in ministry. For the happily dispensable pastor, her constant presence and functioning is unnecessary. She is happy that her congregation can flourish when she is out of town on vacation or out of the office on her day off. As dispensable, she also "travels well," influencing others by her wisdom and professionalism long after she has gone. As this American Baptist pastor notes, "Only God is indispensable. My job is to help people be faithful to God's call when I'm not around. Like a good parent, a good pastor gives her congregation both roots and wings."

The pastor who has learned the wisdom of graceful imperfection and the art of dispensability may become the most effective leader over the long haul precisely because she trusts God to provide her congregation and herself with a vision of possibility and the energy to achieve it. In trusting the lay leaders, she allows them breathing space from which their own leadership styles and sense of responsibility will emerge.

Taking Responsibility for Your Own Health

For Tim, a United Methodist pastor in his early fifties, the primary issue of autumnal personal transformation involved changing his lifestyle to support his own personal well-being. "When I hit fifty, I felt the first real signs of my mortality. I knew that if I didn't begin a regular exercise program and find ways to respond to the stresses of ministry, I'd be facing a future of hypertension, heart disease, and disability, given my family's medical history." Although Tim admits that he didn't initially want to begin an exercise program, seeing himself in his daughter's wedding pictures challenged him to embrace a lifestyle of physical, spiritual, and relational well-being. "I exercise regularly now. Sometimes I even do my pastoral calls on foot or make a walking date with the chair of the board to go over business for the congregational board. I've found a meditative prayer that speaks to my personality type. I read Scripture and then take time to be still for fifteen minutes every morning as I drink my morning coffee. Actually, I've even cut down on caffeine. Now, I'm twenty pounds lighter and feel twenty years younger," rejoices this pastor who is beginning his twenty-first year in ministry.

Integrated wholeness of mind, body, spirit, and relationships is at the heart of biblical spirituality. While Jesus did not counsel a particular pathway to health and wholeness, the breadth of Jesus's healing ministry reflected his concern with enabling people to live God's abundant life spiritually, socially, and physically. Today, pastors can take consolation in the growing interest in spirituality, health, and wholeness in congregational life. Parish nursing and hands-on healing arts such as reiki and healing touch are commonplace in many mainstream congregations. If, as current medical research suggests, prayer is good medicine and congregational involvement is a factor in overall good health and longevity, then pastors had better be challenged to take their own health seriously, especially in midlife.[14]

The encounter of Elijah and Naaman provides an example of one pathway to wellness in midlife. When Naaman, a foreign general suffering from a skin ailment, hears that all he has to do to regain his health is to dip himself in the nearest river, he becomes angry at the prophet. He can't believe that the pathway to healing is right in front of him. He finds wholeness and healing when he embraces the simplest of all practices, dipping himself in the Jordan (2 Kings 5:1-14).

The same is true for many pastors, who forget that health and wholeness in midlife are simply a matter of following certain basic practices of well-being, which include regular physician visits, exercise, a diet appropriate to one's health and body type, adequate sleep, sabbath time, days off, stress reduction, and meditation. For many of us in midlife, the path of good health involves the right balance of meditation and medication, eating and exercise, and play and prayer. Mindful healthy living enables us not only to prevent serious illness but also to experience greater energy and effectiveness in our own lives. Once again, intentionality and regularity complement a commitment to transformation and novelty in ministry. While both of us practice a number of the healthy habits for mind, body, and spirit that we describe in this chapter, we speak as pastors "in process" as we face our own struggles with weight, high blood pressure, and high cholesterol.

Today a growing number of pastors are discovering that their own personal pathways to health also promote excellence in ministry. Suzanne regularly takes what she calls a "preaching walk." After reflecting on the lectionary readings for the week, she puts on her walking shoes and hits the trail for an hour of exercise. Sometimes she lets her mind wander as she feasts on the beauty of nature; but she also carries a small tape recorder to preserve surprising insights that often become the basis for the Sunday sermon. "During my Monday morning walk, I experience the joy of ministry. As I behold the wonders of Mother Nature, I feel a sense of peace that opens the door to inspiration. Sometimes the insights come so easily that I have the outline of the sermon in my mind by the time I return home." Often depleted by his pastoral encounters, David regularly experiences the runner's high as he jogs through the county park near his home. David finds that this time of lively, athletic introversion charges him up for his evening pastoral calls and board meetings. "I simply need to be away from everything for half an hour each day. A nice jog energizes me for my family and for the work that lies ahead."

One of the gifts of midlife often experienced by pastors is the simple discovery that God's passion for abundant life applies to them as well as to their parishioners. As one pastor relates, "It took me nearly twenty years of ministry to realize that my effectiveness as a pastor is connected with my health and happiness. When I take time to exercise, pray, play with my grandchildren, and enjoy the company of my wife, my life and ministry are renewed. I'm so glad I have a job that gives me the flexibility to go home for an afternoon walk with my wife or just spending some time doing prayerful reading in the midst of a fifty-hour week." Although aging occurs despite all our efforts toward health and wholeness, midlife can mean greater happiness and better health for pastors who joyfully embrace their whole lives as the medium for revealing God's love.

Longing for a Wellspring in the Wilderness

For most of us, our pathways to wholeness are circuitous. Our spiritual lives, like the seasons of the year, involve seedtime and harvest, but also they also include monsoons and droughts, gentle breezes and hurricane winds. For a while we may live in the glow of spiritual illumination. We may experience Jesus walking beside us and guiding our every step, as Kate did after her born-again experience of accepting Jesus as her personal Savior. At such times, inspiration may come easily and transformation painlessly. Out of such experiences, pastors can be consoled that they were called to ministry, like Esther, for "just such a time as this." But, then, out of nowhere, they can find themselves in the wilderness with no clear direction. The voice of God so present when they heard their call to ministry or the romance of their first congregational appointment may be suddenly or gradually eclipsed by deep spiritual silence.

When old images of God die or when a pastor has lost the freshness of God's intimacy that characterized the springtime of ministry, he fears that God has abandoned him altogether. He wonders when, or if, a new vision of God will emerge. As a spiritual child of the ancient shaman, a pastor may panic and wonder how she can continue leading worship or preaching each week when she no longer experiences theological clarity or experiential illumination of her initial sense of call. On the journey through the rough, uncharted spiritual wilderness, a pastor wonders if she or he will ever experience the joy and certainty that characterized God's call to ministry. Such feelings of spiritual desolation and abandonment are no strangers to those who take the Psalms with them on their spiritual journeys.

> As a deer longs for flowing streams,
> so my soul longs for you, O God.
> My soul thirsts for God,
> for the living God.
> When shall I come and behold
> the face of God?
> My tears have been my food
> day and night,
> while people say to me continually,
> "Where is your God?"
> —Psalm 42:1-3

Such dark nights of the ministerial spirit can be the death knell of a pastor's career, but they can also be the womb of becoming, from which new and deeper faith and sense of self in ministry may emerge. One may, with the psalmist, trust that the changing seasons will eventually give birth to a new vision of God and a more mature and universal experience of the holy. "Hope in God; for I shall again praise [God], my help and my God" (Ps. 42:11). But, in the midst of spiritual and vocational dry spells there is no guarantee that refreshment and clarity will come.

Noted pastor and Hebrew Bible scholar Renita Weems describes her own journey through the wilderness in *Listening for God: A Pastor's Journey through Silence and Doubt*. In the midst of her growing notoriety as a lecturer in spirituality, Weems found herself spiritually depleted. Weems notes that "I was feeling that God had withdrawn from me and I was going through what I can only describe as a spiritual breakdown—questioning seriously my belief in God, prayer, religious texts, and rituals to such a degree that I couldn't bear to talk or read about anything to do with the sacred."[15]

Weems's experience is not unusual for pastors in midcareer. In a retreat on healing at Kirkridge, a retreat and study center in the Pocono Mountains of eastern Pennsylvania, Kate was surprised to hear Morton Kelsey, an Episcopalian priest and noted author and leader in the area of healing and spirituality, confess that during a time of deep depression and spiritual absence, he was so spiritually depleted that he often depended on his wife to write his sermons. More recently, the writings of Mother Teresa of Calcutta reveal that even a "saint" can go through a period of doubt and depression.[16]

John, the pastor of a large Presbyterian congregation experienced God's absence as "the death of theological certainty." "Influenced by Barth and Calvin and committed to the authority of Scripture, my certainties were shattered when I truly internalized the horrible suffering of the Holocaust and the pain that some of my parishioners were experiencing as a result of profound physical and mental illness. The all-powerful and transcendent God of my seminary training no longer made sense to me. I felt like I was in a theological wasteland with no clear destination. I realized I could no longer worship the God of power and might. I couldn't even say the word *almighty* in the liturgy anymore. For a while, I thought of leaving the congregational ministry and going into pastoral counseling." His salvation as a pastor occurred, first, in a theological encounter with Paul Tillich's *Dynamics of Faith*, where he was reminded that vital faith embraced doubt. His theological framework became even more expanded when he discovered process theology's image of divine power as imaginative and persuasive rather than coercive and omnipotent. "When the God of my first twenty years of ministry died, I found a new vision of God that I could preach with conscience and excitement. A God who feels my pain and invites me to share in the redeeming of the world speaks to my need to confront evil in all its forms, knowing that God is in the fight with me. If I hadn't persisted in looking for a new theological path, I believe I would have eventually left congregational ministry."

Much like Kate, after a decade of ministry, Judy discovered that she could no longer believe in the predominately male and heterosexual imagery that characterized her congregation's liturgical and spiritual practices. Although she had studied feminist theology and used inclusive language in seminary, she had capitulated to the hierarchical and masculine language that was normative in the congregations she served. Only later did Judy discover that by turning her back on feminine images of God she eventually stifled her pastoral imagination and sense of God's accompanying nearness. No longer able to invoke solely the Father God with integrity, Judy struggled to find integrity in both her private and public prayer and devotional life. In her own theological wilderness, Judy found bread for the journey through a women's spiritual direction group. For a while she continued to use the traditional liturgies even though she could no longer assent to the realities they described. When she gathered the strength to speak of God as mother as well as father, Judy discovered that "God was alive again. I had been using the wrong words and knocking on the wrong doors for so long that I almost couldn't find my way back home. But when the Spirit gave me a new language, she also gave me a new heart for preaching and for prayer. I now know that for some persons the male imagery for God provides comfort and protection, but not for me. My living God is 'mother' and 'father' and 'sister' and 'brother.' I can pray again! God is right here in my heart, midwifing me to the next horizons of my journey of faith."

In midcareer, Roger found himself in the wilderness when he discovered that despite all his theological training and commitment to social action, he had never truly experienced God in a personal and intimate way. "While my ministry was successful, I was astounded when I realized it was all head and hands, with no heart. I had heard about the Christian mystics but, frankly, they frightened me. In seminary, I felt that the spirituality courses were too experiential and fluffy compared to the analytic orientation of the courses in Scripture and theology. I wanted to be in control of my spiritual life. But what I found out was that without a sense of God's intimate presence, the words grew stale and the actions frustrating. I was simply going through the motions each Sunday as I preached a gospel and spoke words of prayer that I never really experienced." Recognizing that his spiritual depletion might be an invitation toward personal and professional transformation, Roger sought out a spiritual director who had background in theology and philosophy. They regularly met for silence, theological sharing, and spiritual reflection. Roger notes, "I'm glad I found a spiritual director who could match me intellectually. I realize now that spiritual direction is an intimate process in which there needs to be a close intellectual and experiential match between the director and the directee." While Roger still is energized by the life of the mind, he now feels in touch with the presence of the Spirit and more integrated emotionally in his ministry. His theologically sound sermons and socially responsible activism are now balanced by his regular attention to prayer, personal experience, and the surprises of God's spirit.

These pastors, like Renita Weems, all could have quit ministry. But they found staying power through a combination of patience, endurance, and commitment to personal transformation. They reached out for support and found solace in practicing the pastoral rituals of the church until God became real in a new way.

In the unsettledness of her own personal wilderness, Weems found her way in the historical practices of ministry, worship, and spirituality. She chose to stay in ministry and remain active as a congregational pastor, preacher, and worship leader, despite her spiritual dryness. "It dawned on me that ministry was precisely where I needed to be *because* I no longer recognized the presence of God in my life."[17] Like Weems, the pastors whose testimonies are found in this section continued to lead worship, pray with the sick, administer the sacraments, and speak of faith *until* God became real again for them. They trusted that the God who called them in their youth would be with them in the wilderness of spiritual desolation. They were also willing to change their perception of God's presence by committing themselves to serious theological reflection and questioning.

In reflecting on his experience of grief following the death of his wife, C. S. Lewis noted that grief and loss are essential seasons of every good marriage. At midlife in ministry, doubt, uncertainty, and spiritual depletion are also important seasons in the life of ministry. As Renita Weems notes, the greatest pain in her spiritual life has been "the result of my failure to surrender to the season in which I found myself."[18] Surrender is not passivity but the choice to accept one's current spiritual experience as a window into the fullness of God's nature and an opportunity to experience God in new and adventurous ways. These pastors are now flourishing in ministry because they committed themselves to personal transformation even though God appeared silent and the path ahead uncertain. Today these pastors rejoice in the discovery that "the light at the end of the tunnel isn't always an oncoming train!" They affirm that God was quietly and gently inspiring them toward wholeness and pastoral vitality despite God's apparent absence.

Discovering Your First Love in Ministry

Although Sharon had been the successful senior pastor of a midsized city congregation for ten years, she often felt overwhelmed by the seemingly endless administrative tasks that greeted her with each new day. Instead of beginning her work day with prayer and pastoral care, she usually had to respond to the administrative crisis of the moment. Looking back on her ministry, Sharon notes that "after several years, I grew tired of being the CEO of a small organization, managing bricks and mortar, hypersensitive employees, and mediating between the congregation and the day care center on a daily basis. I knew I was doing good work, and that many of my colleagues would have loved to be in my shoes. But I was missing the love that brought me to ministry—the simple tasks of pastoral care, time spent with children and their parents, and meeting people in times of celebration and grief." After several months of prayerful reflection in companionship with her spiritual director, Sharon accepted a call to pastor a smaller congregation in a town of five thousand people. As she recalls, "Some of my colleagues thought I was crazy. They couldn't understand how I could leave the fast track to a 'big steeple church' for a congregation of one-hundred-fifty members whose budget was barely one-hundred-thousand dollars." Today Sharon relishes her small town ministry. "I am finally doing what I was called to do. I meet folks on the street and in the middle of talking about the weather, they share their hearts with me. I spend three mornings a week drinking coffee and meeting folks at the local cafe. Sure, it's no Starbucks, and there are problems, but we solve them face to face, giving and taking, and always end with a prayer. This is ministry for me." In midlife, with over fifteen years of pastoral experience, Sharon rediscovered her first love. She took a less traveled road and found novelty amid the simplicity of day-to-day ministry in small town America.

Alice was a hardworking United Church of Christ pastor who led her congregation to new adventures in mission and to becoming a congregation that is "open and affirming" toward gay, lesbian, bisexual, and transgendered persons. But in her tenth year, she felt the call of another love, her family of origin. Her father had been diagnosed with Alzheimer's disease and her mother was finding it more and more difficult to care for him. The decision wasn't easy, but Alice also took a novel path in ministry—she left her established congregation to take a small, ecumenical church on the outskirts of

Albuquerque, New Mexico. "It was my turn to care for my parents, who had done so much for me. I made sacrifices but the gifts I have received in supporting my parents are greater than I could have imagined." Alice embodies the counsel that a judicatory official gave to another pastor whose father had also been diagnosed with Alzheimer's: "Your family is also your ministry. Take care of them with the same love and patience that you give an elder adult in your congregation."

After a decade at an established small town congregation, Ed chose to accept a call to a congregation that adjoins a large state university. As he pondered the call, Ed realized that he had hidden many of his gifts and passions from his small town congregation. Although Ed and his family had loved the simplicity of small town America, they often had to be careful in sharing their more liberal political beliefs, concern for social justice, and interest in global spirituality. Midlife called Ed to greater honesty in ministry when he began to circulate his ministerial profile. During his interview with the congregation that eventually called him to be its pastor, Ed was clear that he needed to be himself in ministry. He wanted to match his gifts with the congregation's greatest needs in a way that preserved his own integrity as a progressive and global Christian. He was delighted when he found out that this new congregation had a history of interfaith dialogue, shared a yearly Passover seder with a local Jewish congregation, and had been a leader in marriage equality and social justice in the community. "Now I can do ministry as a whole person," Ed proclaims. "I participate in a weekly meditation group and help lead a book group that focuses on texts in emerging and progressive Christianity and social change. I can be myself, honestly sharing my vision of faith, whether in the pulpit, a study group, or a personal conversation." With nearly twenty years of ministerial experience, Ed has never been so energized and excited about his role as pastor.

When pastors rediscover their spiritual passions and are able to integrate them into their day-to-day ministries, miracles happen for pastors and congregations. New energies are released and new possibilities emerge. Experienced pastors begin to see their vocation and their personal lives in a whole new light.

If you are in the autumn of your ministry, as you ponder the vitality of your ministry, where is your current passion? What is your first love? Are you living out of your deepest vocational and spiritual gifts? Or are you hiding your light under a bushel basket? What do you need to do to experience greater vital energy and inspiration within your day-to-day ministry?

Transforming Relationships

Despite the growing emphasis on lay leadership and nonhierarchical ministry, most pastors still remain at the hub of dynamic and interdependent congregational life. How they relate to the individuals in the congregation profoundly affects the health of the congregational system. Unhealthy pastors, unable to develop healthy relationships inside or outside the congregation, to establish regular self-care disciplines and spiritual practices, or to maintain firm professional boundaries, contribute significantly to congregational dysfunction. Vital congregations, with transformational visions, recognize and affirm issues of wellness and health among their leaders, lay or clergy. In the spirit of this text, ministerial renewal and transformation are intimately connected to intentional and transforming relationships. In what follows, we will describe three models of collegial support and transformation.

The Alliance for the Renewal of Ministry

Lancaster Theological Seminary's Renewing Ministry program, like all of the seminary's ministerial excellence and transformation programs, is grounded in two Pauline affirmations:

> The one who began a good work among you will bring it to completion by the day of Jesus Christ . . . having produced the

harvest of righteousness that comes through Jesus Christ for the glory and praise of God.

—Philippians 1:6, 11

Do not be conformed to this world, but be transformed by the renewing of your minds, so that you may discern what is the will of God—what is good and acceptable and perfect.

—Romans 12:2

Initiated through a grant from the Lilly Endowment in 1998, the Alliance for the Renewal of Ministry, now known as Renewing Ministry, was the first of Lancaster Theological Seminary's ministerial excellence programs. Similar to the Wholeness in Ministry program for new pastors, the Renewing Ministry program brings together experienced pastors with more than five years in ministry for collegial reflection, sharing, spiritual formation, and study. Grounded in the recognition that renewal and transformation occur in the interplay of solitude and community, Renewing Ministry joins prayerful reflection and sharing with thematic studies aimed at enabling experienced pastors to see their lives and ministries in new ways. Each group charts its course, based on the interplay of the program's vision and their own personal needs and goals. Over the years, groups have focused on themes such as healing ministry, congregational conflict, postmodern evangelism, spiritual practices for pastors, preaching and worship in various liturgical seasons, God's current call in my ministry, dealing with transitions in life and ministry, appreciative inquiry for congregational visioning, stewardship, death and bereavement, and evangelism. Each theme is framed in such a way that it reflects the experiences of the participants, provides tools for congregational growth, and deepens pastoral spirituality.

Over the three- to four-year lifespan of each group, pastors support each other through the challenges and transitions of midcareer ministry. As one member noted, "Having a group of experienced colleagues was essential in enabling me to realize the toxic patterns of my last congregation. My colleagues reminded me that I wasn't crazy and that, rather than being destroyed by the congregation, I could begin to ponder a new call." The colleague group provided a safe and confidential place for anger, tears, and discernment as well as encouragement for this pastor as he sought, and found, a new call to a much healthier congregation. Another pastor notes that "The group challenged my tendency to overfunction as pastor. One member in particular constantly told me to 'lighten up and get a life' outside the church. It hasn't been easy, but I'm taking steps to get out of the way so that the lay people can do ministry."

Members of these clergy groups accompany one another in facing the death of parents, family issues such as a child's discernment about sexual orientation, congregational resistance to new ideas, and job loss. Transition requires a death of old patterns of ministry and living, and letting go of the familiar can be painful even when new possibilities are emerging. Collegial support provides interpersonal assurance in the wilderness of transition.

Renewing Ministry groups have a generative quality. With the emergence of the Wholeness in Ministry program for pastors in their first congregational call, experienced pastors from within Renewing Ministry colleague groups have assumed roles as co-leaders and mentors for the new pastors involved in the program. As one leader confesses, "Being with new pastors helps me see my work with new eyes, and sharing my gifts and experience enables me to be part of something larger, the future of ministry, as well as to claim the goodness of my own life as a pastor."

Informal Accountability and Partnership Groups

While many pastors are tempted to be lone rangers, others realize that they cannot go it alone. An ecumenical group of pastors in western Maryland meets one morning each month for prayer, Scripture, and mutual support and accountability. Although informal groups do not have institutional support, they operate according to the same principles of safety, confidentiality, and care

as found in more formal groups. Over the years informal accountability groups have clearly helped pastors deal with congregational
crises and resistance; they also have called their members to the
highest ministerial values. As one member notes, "I'm not alone.
Somebody's praying for me and cares enough to challenge me and
tell me when I'm hurting myself or my congregation. I'm not sure
I could make it in ministry without this group."

More flexible theme-based groups, such as lectionary study
groups, gather around a theme such as preaching but soon discover
that preaching and liturgy can't be separated from issues of family,
professional life, and congregational health. Members implicitly
come to realize that the pastor's spiritual and family life can't be
separated from her or his preaching and that unstructured or
informal moments of prayer and support provide bread for the
journey, especially for pastors whose ministry occurs far from the
intellectual and interpersonal resources of seminaries.

A group of three United Church of Canada pastors in Mon-
treal meets regularly to create progressive and creation-centered
devotional materials for their congregations. Their regular meetings and joint creativity has nurtured a synergy that has energized
every aspect of their ministries. Still, it is important to note that
even informal groups should maintain a high standard of personal
support, accountability, and confidentiality.

Coaching for Clergy

When he began his new position as an interim pastor with the
responsibility of guiding the congregational revitalization of a
historical congregation, John knew that he needed someone to
help him stay on track and keep perspective in his challenging
new pastorate. John knew his own wisdom and self-awareness
were pivotal in helping the congregation move from stasis to a vital
future. Accordingly, John sought out the counsel of Val Hastings,
an experienced United Methodist pastor whose own vocational
journey had led him from pastoral ministry to clergy coaching.

As an experienced pastor, John was perceptive enough to know the pitfalls of ministry in midlife. But it was important for John to have a vision that helped him prioritize the day-to-day tasks of ministry and to stay fresh and flexible in times of challenge and resistance. John's regular work with his clergy coach enables him to see both the forest and the trees, and to discern what's "truly important in his current ministry."

Regular conversations with his coach challenge John to consciously reflect on "what I did, what I didn't do, and what got in the way of achieving my goals in ministry." His conversations with Val serve as a professional compass that show him where he's going in ministry, especially in the new terrain of his role as the spiritual leader of a revitalizing congregation. Val's questions and counsel during John's biweekly phone appointments help him constantly ask himself, "Am I going in the right direction? And, if not, how can I get back on the right path?" Like any good coach, Val helps John gain greater self-awareness in his practice of ministry.

According to Val Hastings, the role of a clergy coach is to be a "catalyst, accelerating what's already there in a pastor's ministry, helping pastors refocus their ministry." The motto of Hastings's work is "heads up, heads down." Coaching enables pastors "to go from the daily grind of ministry to imaging a larger perspective." When pastors appear stuck in old habits or reach dead ends in their professional ministry, clergy coaching helps them respond to the question, "How do we go forward?"[19]

In her own pastoral journey, Kate sought the informal coaching of an experienced pastor, Robert Perry, when she was called as senior pastor of the Palisades Community Church. Throughout her ten years in ministry, Kate and Bob met regularly for lunch, conversation, and wise counsel that she admits were essential in helping her stay on track and find perspective in the context of pastoring a growing congregation.

No pastor can flourish without the gift of a larger perspective that enables her or him to see God in the ordinary tasks of ministry. Healthy ministry attests to the wisdom of Paul's image of the body of Christ. Whether through the questioning of a coach, the challenges of an informal accountability group, or the mutual mentoring of an intentional colleague group, vitality and staying power in ministry are the gift of small and large communities of safety, love, and wisdom.

Spiritual Practices for Ministry's Autumn

Use the following assessments, affirmations, and practices to help you with the tasks of endurance and transformation and move you toward wholeness in this season of ministry.

Taking Care of the Temple

As one fifty-year-old pastor noted, "All my life I've been healthy. I've never even had surgery. But now I'm constantly noticing aches and pains. The phrase 'use it or lose it' applies to me, too. I need to be consistent in taking care of myself—in exercising and watching what I eat. I can't take my health for granted anymore." Now a high protein breakfast, eight glasses of water daily, and regular walking each morning have become part of her daily ritual. Another pastor who dealt with chronic obesity has chosen to seize the day and address self-care. "I take time for daily exercise—walking and Pilates—and cross off an hour each day on my schedule for centering prayer. If I get tired in the middle of the day, rather than pushing through with an large cup of coffee like I used to, I close my study door and take a half-hour nap on the sofa. Giving myself permission to rest has been a godsend and a lifesaver. I am eating more fish and less carbohydrates. I have more energy and creativity than I could have imagined before."

Frederick Buechner invites us to listen to our lives. In that spirit, take a moment to listen to your lifestyle. Ask yourself a few simple questions:

1. What is my current weight? Am I overweight or underweight? How would I describe my diet—healthy, unhealthy, intentional, mixed? How do I feel when I eat certain foods? What foods relax me, decrease my energy, or energize me? What foods do I truly enjoy? When and where do I eat?
2. Do I wake up refreshed or tired? What's my typical energy level? Do I drag through the day or have enough energy for work, family, and recreation?
3. What is my current approach to exercise? Do I have an exercise ritual? What exercises feel most comfortable and life giving to me?
4. How would I describe my spiritual life? Do I take time for prayer and meditation? Does prayer inform my ministry or is it an afterthought?
5. Do I sleep well? How many hours of sleep do I get each night? Is that enough? Do I take naps or rest when I need to or drive myself to exhaustion?
6. How would I describe my use of alcohol and other substances? What positive behaviors do I use to relax? What negative behaviors do I use to relax?
7. Do I practice self-care activities such as massage, reiki, the relaxation response, or centering prayer?

Our goal in asking these questions is to encourage self-awareness rather than prescribe a particular dietary, exercise, or lifestyle plan. Such questions invite one to consider ways he or she can practice wholeness in every aspect of life. Taking care of the temple is a matter of inspiration and commitment, passion and balance. Stewardship relates to our time, energy, and embodiment as well as to our financial resources and care for the planet. If God is revealed intimately in our bodies, then we are challenged to ask, "How can I glorify God in my body?"

Based on the insights of holistic and complementary medicine and Christian spirituality, make a commitment to regularly practicing a whole person approach to well-being that provides appropriate nurture for your mind, body, and spirit. Scientific research and global wisdom are clear that dynamic health requires a balance of lively activity, hope and imagination, rest and refreshment, meditation and prayer, fresh and healthy food, and a willingness to take responsibility for what is in one's power and to let go of what lies outside of one's control.

Transforming Your Mind through Affirmations

A greeting card on our bedroom mirror highlights a bold proclamation attributed to Christian mystic Evelyn Underhill: "Christ wants not nibblers of the possible but grabbers of the impossible." This statement captures the essence of Paul's counsel, "Do not be conformed to this world, but be transformed by the renewing of your minds" (Rom. 12:2). Midlife reminds a person that she or he must make the best of the limitations inherent in one's previous decisions, roads not taken, relational choices, and the aging process. As many note, this can lead to a spiritual crises, but within the crises a person experiences, she or he may discover the surprises of grace.

Spiritual affirmations—positive statements about God, the universe, and ourselves—awaken and expand the pastoral imagination. They enable one to imagine a larger world and then take the first steps to embodying the world he or she envisages. Spiritual affirmations, repeated regularly throughout the day and in times of challenge, transform both the conscious and the unconscious mind. They serve as theological and spiritual Lysol for negative self-talk and the ever-present negative buzz of detractors and thoughtless gossip within our congregations. They enable us to recover the faithful optimism that led us into ministry. Indeed, the two of us believe that the most insightful theological and creedal statements contain affirmations that transform mind, body, and spirit. These affirmations enable pastors to experience God's deeper presence in the context of congregational conflict, membership decline, culture wars, and professional uncertainty. Affirmations can become the hermeneutic, or lens, through which a person comes to view his or her life as a pastor and congregational leader.

We have found that writing down our affirmations on note cards and consulting them throughout the day is a powerful way of grounding them in everyday decisions and actions. You may also choose to repeat your affirmations at regular intervals throughout the day and in times of crisis and challenge. Bruce advises his seminary students to utilize affirmations as a means of growing into their role as preachers and pastors. For example, one seminary student takes a deep breath and repeats the following affirmation as she comes to the pulpit to preach: "God guides my words so that they inspire others to know the love of Christ." While affirmations do not replace the hard work of study, continuing education, spiritual direction, and therapy, they give us the confidence to see ourselves as we truly are—God's beloved and gifted partners in transforming the world.[20]

Bruce invites seminarians and pastors in their first congregational call to live by affirmations such as:

- God inspires my preaching and teaching. My sermons are inspirational and life changing.
- God is constantly giving me new ideas and insights into effective ministry. I creatively balance the quest for ministerial excellence with a commitment to self-care and healthy relationships.

Scriptural affirmations for ministerial transformation in all the seasons of ministry include the following:

- I am the light of the world. I let my light shine (Matt. 5:14).
- I can do all things through Christ who strengthens me (Phil. 4:13).
- My God will supply all my needs (Phil. 4:19).

Bruce invites pastors in midlife to consider not only the affirmations mentioned above but transforming phrases such as:

- My body is the temple of God, and I take time to care for my physical well-being through exercise, a good diet, rest, and spiritual renewal.
- New ideas are constantly coming to me that will transform my ministry and personal life.
- My age and experience enable me to grow in wisdom and effectiveness in ministry.

Kate finds that her spiritual directees, especially those who are facing crises in their church, experience greater peace when they focus on gentle belly breathing (drawing each breath deeply into the stomach) and then repeat silently over and over, "Nothing can separate me from the love of God in Christ Jesus our Lord" with each breath. They may choose to place a concrete situation in the context of their affirmations, such as, "Congregational conflict cannot separate me from the love of God" or "This budget cannot separate me from the love of God."

Affirmations are practices that transform one's life and ministry. They help create habits that transform and renew one's mind, enabling a person to grow in energy and stature and to see the routine tasks of ministry as windows into the heart of God. We encourage pastors to look deeply into their lives, reflecting on their deepest needs and challenges, and then create spiritual affirmations to respond to these needs. For example, a pastor, whose busyness in ministry pushed her to the edge of burnout, turned her life and ministry around as she began to live with affirmations such as:

- God's grace enables me to let go of perfectionism.
- God is inspiring me to take time for my health and family.
- God loves me whether I succeed or fail in this project.

Another pastor, whose life and ministry were being undermined by a growing sense of personal scarcity as well as concerns about his aging, found peace and new focus in his ministry and personal life by living with these spiritual affirmations. Whenever he felt threatened by low self-esteem, worries about the future, or feelings of inadequacy, he repeated affirmations such as:

- I have all the time, energy, and money to do what I truly need to do for God, my family, myself, and this congregation.
- Wherever I go, God is with me.
- I am God's beloved son, in whom God is pleased.

While affirmations do not magically change one's circumstances or create a unilateral field of force that immediately brings success and abundance into a person's life, they expand one's personal and pastoral imagination in such a way that one can envisage new possibilities, discover solutions to chronic problems, and feel peace amid the challenges of ministry. A transformed mind leads to transformed decision-making processes and new and creative encounters.

Initiating Novelty Personally and Professionally

The twin ministerial virtues of midlife are endurance and transformation. When pursued with discipline, these two virtues integrate the polarities of order and novelty. Too much order leads to stagnation, while too much novelty leads to chaos. In art and ministry, creative transformation involves the right balance of order and novelty. The tendency of many experienced pastors is to err on the side of order—that is, to repeat good habits of ministry and effective leadership practices year after year. At times, however, these practices no longer nurture the pastor's imagination, spiritual life, or leadership in the congregation.

Growing and effective pastors are proactive in initiating novelty, rather than waiting for the congregation to thrust it upon them. At every season of ministry, growing pastors look for the changes going on in their congregations and in society and creatively anticipate changes to come, developing strategic skills and sensitivities for potential growth areas in themselves and in their congregations and communities.

The ability to anticipate changes and initiate novelty in personal, congregational, and community life is primarily a matter of attention and openness to God's presence in our constantly changing world. Pastors who initiate novelty in their lives, congregations, and communities regularly cultivate what the philosopher Søren Kierkegaard described as a "passion for the possible." They expect the unexpected and have resources to respond when surprises occur. Accordingly, in every situation, they look for the seeds of possibility and creativity, grounded in God's vision of the future. Mindful of the present moment, they also discern where the spirit of the moment may be leading. They consciously choose to be aligned with God's aim at shalom for themselves, their congregations, and the wider community.

Yet, how does a pastor cultivate this spirit of creative transformation, or spiritual initiative? First, we have found that pastors need to nurture the practices of prayer, meditation, and mindfulness as they relate to pastors' personal lives. As you look at your life and ministry, where do you hear God's voice calling you forward? Where do you hear new and creative voices in your congregation? What new ideas or practices are waiting to be born? You may choose to journal your responses to these questions or draw or paint a picture of the emerging future that you anticipate. Imagine yourself as a dynamic actor and leader in shaping the present and future flow of life within your congregation and community, in partnership with God and those with whom you minister.

Second, pastors who cultivate a spirit of creative transformation pause to notice what's really going on in the life of the church as they ask, "What are the spiritual currents at work in my congregation? Where do I see God's mission emerging in this congregation?" They ask for guidance as they imagine where these spiritual currents might lead, should the congregation choose to pursue new possibilities for faithfulness.

Third, these pastors listen to God's presence in culture as well as the church. Recognizing that the boundary between church and culture is permeable, they look for the signs of the times among seekers of all ages and cultural movements and in the media. In so doing, they choose to say yes to the novel by having an attitude of openness to change and diversity.

As you experience the words, art, and music of other generational age groups (Generation X, twenty-somethings, millennials, boomers, senior adults), what spiritual yearnings do you experience? If you really listened to the deeper rhythms of other generations, where would you be called to change your approach to ministry? What skills and practices of other age and ethnic groups can you explore and learn in your quest for faithful ministry?

What new ministerial leadership actions would you need to take if you listened to God's ongoing revelations in your life, in the congregation, and in other generations? What risks would you need to take? What new possibilities would you need to midwife to respond or to move ahead of the changes in your world?

Covenant of Spiritual Transformation for Autumn in Ministry

The quest to embody a ministry of endurance and vitality calls experienced pastors to stay fresh and ahead of the game in their ministries and personal lives. The interplay of staying power and ongoing freshness requires a deep intentionality, reflected in the following covenants of spiritual transformation:

- I covenant to become aware of God's call to transformation in my life and congregation.
- I make a commitment to explore and embody new approaches to my ministry and relationships.

- I commit myself to pursuing ongoing continuing education that will nurture mind, body, spirit, relationships, the arts, and professional life.

⟨ 5 ⟩

Winter in Ministry
Vision and Letting Go

On the Monday after his retirement, Gordon Forbes knew that if he didn't have a plan for the day, he would get in his car after breakfast and it would automatically drive to Westmoreland Church of Christ, just as it had done for nearly twenty years. Instead, he intentionally drove in the other direction, toward scenic Harpers Ferry, where he sat on a rock and wrote this poem.

Down Stream at Harpers Ferry

I watch thirty ninth graders board the shuttle-
field trip to the National Park.
They'll learn of Union and Confederate maneuvers,
hear of cannon, rifles, insurrection.

I will ignore this history today.
I feel pulled toward the river
to a rock at the spot
where legs of two rivers meet.

The wind peels leaves,
just past peak, twirls them
to rushing currents. River
receives their fluttering, carries them
downstream. Rocks, and whirlpools
ahead, the tumble over Great Falls,
headed for the bay. Conception,
birth, death converge.

The white spire of St. Peter's church
juts like a needle above the trees,
points to heaven. But I have not come
for heaven. I come to watch the leaves,
just past peak, get carried away to
places they cannot imagine on
this first day of my retirement.[1]

At first glance, winter is a season of starkness and retreat. As we look out on the grove of trees behind our home in Lancaster, Pennsylvania, on a winter morning, their bare limbs look lifeless. Compared to the colorful birthings of springtime, the lush greenings of summer, and the vibrant red and golden hues of autumn, winter grays and whites seem drab and stagnant. But lingering a bit as we look again, we notice the beauty of uniquely shaped branches and limbs, and when snow laden, their frosting calls us to a tranquility that inspires a sense of sabbath solitude. More than that, now that the leaves, so lush and colorful in summer and autumn, have fallen into warm mulch, insulating the earth, we can, for the first time in several months, see the gentle twinkle of our neighbor's lights one hundred yards up the hill. Their presence is warm and inviting and draws us closer as neighbors. Somehow the starkness makes way for vision and perspective. Like the bare terrain of the Scottish Highlands or the Isle of Iona, winter has a beauty all its own.

Walking through Bushnell Park in Hartford, Connecticut, at sunrise during the General Synod of the United Church of Christ, Bruce synchronously encountered Fred, a retired United Church of Christ pastor. The encounter was synchronous for two reasons: first, Bruce had been planning to call Fred, a multiple-staff pastor who had retired three years before from a historic Maryland congregation, to talk about his retirement experience; and, second, at that very moment as he was walking, Bruce was reflecting on a recent conversation he had had with another retired pastor, who described his first few months of retirement as similar to "walking through a wilderness, moving ahead with no certainty of where the journey would take him." As he pondered his own retirement just over a decade away, Bruce wondered, "Did all pastors have this experience, and, if so, how did they find 'manna in the wilderness' for the next steps of their personal and professional adventures?"

As they walked along together, Bruce asked Fred about his experience of retirement. "I thought it would be a disaster, but it's been a joy," Fred responded. One of the great benefits, Fred noted, about being retired is that now "I can take a long walk each morning, sit down for a cup of coffee at a local restaurant, and then walk home without worrying about being late for an appointment." Fred added that "walking each morning has been essential not only for my physical well-being, but also for my spirit and emotions." After two years of visiting other congregations, Fred mentioned that he was returning as a member to the congregation where he had been senior pastor for twenty-seven years and where a number of his family members belonged. The current senior pastor, secure in her own abilities and confident in Fred's professional integrity, welcomed his return. After forty years of service to the church as a minister, Fred was happy to be a committed layperson in the congregation. Like Gordon Forbes, Fred had no intention of serving another congregation, even for an interim period. He reported that despite initial misgivings, his life in retirement was full of projects and family activities. Fred clearly had a future and a hope beyond full-time ministry.

Susan, a pastor whose congregation is just a few miles north of Fred's Maryland home, reveals that she is pondering her upcoming retirement. With more than twenty years of experience in congregational ministry, and an equal number of years spent before that as an active layperson who because of her gender did not initially see ordained ministry as a viable option, Susan is looking forward to retiring "while I still have plenty of energy." The pastor of a small country church that is slowly becoming surrounded by suburban sprawl, Susan has faithfully provided pastoral leadership, spiritual encouragement, and stable ministry in times of challenge and transition. As she looks toward retirement in a year, Susan believes that she has built a healthy membership and financial foundation for the congregation's ministerial transition when she leaves. As she looks toward her own future, Susan is hopeful. Like Fred, she has many interests she wants to pursue, ranging from low-cost housing for senior adults to knitting. In her retirement, Susan plans to integrate service to the community with a cottage industry in sweater making. Not content with hiding her light under a bushel, Susan is looking forward to supply preaching as well as mentoring younger pastors in the area. Like many experienced pastors approaching retirement, Susan believes that her calling is to be a wisdom giver, sharing her faith, expertise, and practical experience with the next generations of ministers.

The pastor of a one-thousand-member congregation located in central Pennsylvania, John chose to retire at sixty-four, a year earlier than he had originally planned. His rationale was honest and straightforward: "Of course, I'm still doing good ministry, and could have hung in for another year. But, frankly, I would have been doing maintenance ministry. This church needs to move ahead. It needs an experienced interim who is able to ask hard questions and make difficult decisions with the church that I could not do in my final year." Like Gordon Forbes, John sees retirement as a spiritual issue involving letting go of the past, reframing his vocation, and opening to new interests—in John's case, music, foreign languages, and mathematics. Still healthy in mind and body, John plans, after a few years, to enter interim ministry with a focus on multiple-staff congregations. "I am looking forward to living in new places, especially interesting places, where my unique gifts and experience as senior pastor of a large congregation will be an asset."

A Living History

One thing that a pastor contemplating retirement has is a personal and professional history. Author Marilynne Robinson's John Ames, the seventy-year-old Congregationalist minister and protagonist in *Gilead,* describes what it is like to look back at a ministerial career spanning several decades: "My father always preached from notes, and I wrote my sermons out word for word. There are boxes of them in the attic, a few recent years of them in stacks in the closet. . . . Pretty nearly my whole life's work is in those boxes, which is an amazing thing to reflect upon. . . . Say, fifty sermons a year for forty-five years. . . . Two thousand two hundred and fifty [sermons]."[2]

As you look back on your ministry, how many sermons are in your sermon "barrel" or computer file? After his father's death, Bruce pored over the box in which hundreds of his father's sermons were stacked neatly in notebooks binding 4 x 6 inch stationery, a lifetime of Sundays in ministry. Imagine how many pages you have written in the course of your ministry. For those pastors who write out their sermons, we estimate that a twenty-minute sermon fills seven, 8-1/2 x 11 inch, double-spaced computer pages, amounting to more than three hundred pages each year for an every Sunday pastor. Over forty years, that amounts to twelve thousand pages of sermons! This is surely a testament to fidelity and persistence as well as to creativity and inspiration.

Other pastors look at their ministry as healing encounters. Kate counts her thirty-year history of ministry by those with whom she walked in pivotal moments of their lives, such as dying, grief, addiction, unexpected pregnancy, or personal crisis. Kate is grateful for the moments in which her ministry may have meant the difference between life and death. "Preaching is important and I aim at excellence," Kate affirms, "but healing is more important, and that's what I've prized in ministry through the years."

A Time for Lasts

In many ways a minister's retirement is the reverse image of her or his first congregational call. Decades earlier, he or she walked to the pulpit with fear and trembling, about to preach her or his first sermon without the safety net of the seminary community or a field education supervisor. Now, hundreds of sermons and worship services later, when he or she walks to the pulpit for the last time as a full-time congregational pastor, he or she is filled with a different type of fear and trembling, the fear of letting go of a personal identity and theological practice that have defined her or his life for decades. While few pastors at retirement miss board meetings and budget sessions, the quotidian practices that structured her or his life day by day and month by month are what pastors often miss the most.

All transitions require saying goodbye, but some farewells are heart wrenching. When an elderly widow a retiring pastor has visited week after week for more than a decade asks, "Will you come back again next week to see me?" even the most self-differentiated and intentional pastor is tempted to reply, "Of course, I'll be back next week." When a pastor celebrates his last nursing home service and announces that he won't be back again, the anguished looks from the residents are heartbreaking.

The caretaking and wisdom-giving void that follows these pastoral lasts is accompanied by a wide variety of feelings: For some, the feeling of relief at never having to chair another church session meeting or endure the petty conflicts of the church board triumphs over the void and its related grief. Others experience a new freedom at not having to prepare or deliver another sermon designed to light a fire beneath "God's frozen chosen." Yet, for most pastors, the feelings of loss and ambivalence are tremendous because, despite the challenges of ministry, most pastors see a close relationship between what has been described as "soul and role."[3] They do not simply *do* ministry, they *are* ministers 24/7. Their vocation is a matter of character, lifestyle, and self-definition, even if they have healthy family lives, relationships outside the church, and interests outside ministry. Healthy preretirement pastors remind themselves that their choice to respond to God's call to a lifetime of ministry has enabled God to be present in their lives and the lives of their congregants in unique and surprising ways, and they remember that God is still calling them toward faithful discipleship, albeit in yet unknown forms beyond congregational ministry.

Although the philosopher Alfred North Whitehead appropriately affirmed that religion is what a person does with her or his solitariness, the two of us believe that it is equally true that faith and vocation are profoundly defined and shaped by relationships.[4] With retirement from full-time ministry, most pastors note that their relational world suddenly shrinks. Happily, phone calls no longer disturb family meals. But, sadly, days and weeks may go by without a phone call from persons who were once former colleagues or congregants. With no church office filled with congregational staff and volunteers to go to each morning, recent retirees often make visits to the coffee shop or corner restaurant to fill their days. As one suburban pastor noted, "My husband and I decided to retire in the home where we'd lived for two decades. Our children and grandchildren all lived within half an hour of home and the church we'd served for twenty years. I'm glad to be near family, but it's painful to remain so near my old congregation. Sometimes it hurts to see former parishioners sharing lunch with the interim pastor at places that we once shared meals. As I pick up an afternoon coffee at Starbucks, I encounter my successor, former colleagues, and former parishioners, and while I'm tempted to sit down beside them, I know I have to wave and take my coffee on the road. I've had to let go of a congregation when I moved to another, but leaving my job and not having to go to another is heart wrenching. It's difficult even to find a place to eat where I won't encounter someone from the church." With retirement from full-time congregational ministry, one pathway of life comes to an end, and developing new pathways and possibilities takes considerable effort.

The "lasts" of ministry's winter season reminds us of the importance of work in shaping our personal identity prior to retirement and after it. According to students of the psychology of retirement, a person's work serves a variety of psychological and structural functions in her or his life, including a sense of personal worth and accomplishment, relationships and friendships, prestige and recognition, novelty and creativity, service to the larger community, and the passing of time.[5] From a holistic perspective on ministerial vocation in which being and doing are intimately related, the high degree of unsettledness pastors experience as they contemplate their retirement is normal, especially during the first months following their departure from full-time ministry. Even pastors well-versed in boundary training are tempted to quite innocently violate boundaries in order to hang on to some sense of their old identity. There are great temptations to drop in at the office on the way to the market or stop by the women's or men's fellowship group during its monthly meeting in the social hall. But after a few minutes of mutual awkwardness, the retired pastor and his former colleagues and parishioners know that it is time to go. As one recently retired United Church of Christ pastor noted, "It's a humbling and somewhat alienating experience to know that you no longer belong in a place where you were once the center of action and the primary actor. More than that, your presence in the area may be seen by judicatory officials and the new pastor as an intrusion, undermining the authority of your successor. When judicatory officials ask how I'm doing, I feel the underlying message is 'Are you behaving yourself? Are you staying away from the church?'"

Like a flowing stream, life goes on, and our accomplishments, at best, become the foundation upon which other pastors will build in their ministerial adventure. Even those pastors who have prepared well for retirement may experience some wistfulness as they admit that life is progressing well in the office and in the congregation now that they are gone.

"For everything there is a season." Transformation from which new life springs is bought at the price of abandonment of old routines and letting go of old ways of self-definition. The leaves must fall from the tree to create mulch to support springtime's renewal of life. Springtime's new blooms eventually rise but not without the death of the old self and its habitual patterns. In such transitional moments, a pastor's calling is to claim *kairos* time amid the fifty or more unstructured hours of *chronos* time that once defined each week's tasks. What initially seems like a void in the few weeks following retirement may shortly thereafter become the womb of new possibilities for those who awaken to new pathways of spirituality, vocation, and relationship. What the psalmist described as numbering our days will mean embracing the joy of new adventures and new talents, rather than simply passing time in preoccupation with the past.

In Madeleine L'Engle's *A Ring of Endless Light*, Grandfather Austin, a retired Episcopalian priest who is now debilitated and facing immanent death, notes that at this time of his life his vocation is simply to pray for the world.[6] When pastors retire, they do not lose their pastoral identity or their calling to serve God, but their vocation is transformed. Their calling is to discern what new creation God is beckoning them toward now that they no longer have the role of public religious figure. Just as a person's earlier callings have many possible shapes, so, too, God's call in retirement encompasses many paths and possibilities in one's particular time and place.

A Season of Grief and Letting Go

As mentioned earlier, on the first day of his retirement Gordon Forbes fantasized that his car would automatically drive to church as it had done thousands of times before. C. S. Lewis, following his wife's death, describes his grief as an archer aiming at the target, only to realize that the target has been moved.[7] Our thoughts have objects, our trips have destinations, and our days are filled with habitual activities that provide structure and order amid the dynamic processes of life. Without them, we are set adrift.

Just think for a moment about of a pastor's ordinary week. Pastoral practice and imagination is built around activities such as sermon preparation, hospital and home visitation, worship planning, denominational responsibilities, congregational planning, evening board meetings, pastoral care, and staff supervision. While pastors may plan for retirement a year in advance, most pastors move immediately from their on-call, fifty-hour weeks filled with unexpected emergencies and surprises to a schedule that is virtually blank on the day following their retirement celebration. Although some pastors slowly disengage themselves from certain aspects of ministry, such as committee meetings and denominational responsibilities prior to retirement, few pastors, especially solo pastors, have the leisure or the ability to let go of the regular and ongoing administrative and pastoral tasks of ministry prior to their retirement.

Routine defines a person's life, and the importance of routine in self-definition is especially challenging for pastors whose retirement residence, especially in small towns or suburbs, is only a few miles from the congregation they once served. Other pastors, having spent a lifetime living in church parsonages, not only have to quit their jobs but also leave their homes almost immediately after retirement.

No matter the particulars, the freedom of retirement is virtually always accompanied by some form of grief for the loss of order, structure, home, profession, identity, and status that accompanied the vocation of ordained ministry. Again, while the two of us recognize the importance of appropriate boundaries for retired clergy and their families, the surgical approach of excising oneself from a faith community promoted by many ministerial ethicists and judicatory officials often fails to take into consideration the complex relational nature of life and the multiple levels of personal and relational grief that pastors and their spouses experience at retirement. The keeping of healthy boundaries upon leaving a beloved community is easier if one has been intentional about setting one's sight on the next adventure. While healthy boundaries are essential for the well-being of the pastor and community alike, this process is almost always painful and unsettling to those who must leave.

What makes leave taking so challenging is the reality that a pastor's retirement also involves spouses, partners, and children. As one pastor noted, "When I retired, I lost my job and status in the denomination. Colleagues and denominational staff quit calling.

This was painful enough for me, but none of them recognized the grief that my wife experienced when I retired. She had to leave a community of friends that she had come to love deeply during our twenty years of ministry there. My professional life centered on the church, but her personal life and identity were also centered on the church." Our lives are defined by relationships and social groups, and the immediate loss of familiar rituals and close friends that characterizes a pastor's retirement often leaves her or his spouse wondering about her or his own identity as well. The spouse of a pastor who had retired from forty years of ministry, with over twenty years in the final congregation, admitted, "While this may not be the professional norm these days, most of my friends were at church. For twenty years, every Thursday evening I went to choir and every Sunday morning I sang in the choir and taught church school. The women's fellowship was important to my life. I know it's the right thing for me to stay away from church for a year or two. But I feel like a part of me has died. I wonder if I can ever find such a loving community and such good friends."

With retirement comes the loss of a role and title that a pastor has cultivated over as many as twenty to fifty years. "Who will I be when I leave the pulpit?" one pastor asked. "I have a life outside the church. But virtually every waking hour for nearly forty years, the church as been the undercurrent of my life. What will I do when I'm just a regular churchgoer? I'm not even sure I want to go to church for a while when I retire."

Some pastors experience freedom from their ministerial schedules as a second honeymoon and a time to explore new sides of themselves, while others immediately fall into a depression characterized by a sense of aimlessness and fatigue. In either case, celebration and desolation are the prelude to the journey ahead. The retirement adventure is especially important for today's pastors and their families insofar as healthy sixty-five-year-olds can anticipate living twenty to thirty healthy years after they retire. Accordingly, those who seek to have a generative and lively retirement are challenged to follow the example of Gordon Forbes—that is, to seek out the guidance of a spiritual director, therapist, or clergy support group that will enable them to imagine where God will be leading them in the years ahead. We recommend that spouses who have been highly invested in the life of the congregation also seek spiritual direction in order to frame a creative vision of the future.

By definition, winter's transformation requires a high degree of change and loss, just as the prelude to resurrection is always death. Embracing the grief of loss is no easy matter and, in the midst of the wilderness of retirement, we have no guarantees that we will find our promised land. But healthy pastors, along with their partners and spouses, anticipate the grief, feel their pain and loss, and embrace the possibilities for growth that lie within and beyond the wintry wilderness.

Winter Vision Quest

The season of winter can be a time of adventure as well as a time of letting go for pastors. But growth in the winter of ministry is the result of a pastor's willingness to follow faithfully and courageously her or his own spiritual vision into the frontiers of aging and retirement.

Going Forth by Stages

Many pastors considering retirement take solace as well as insight from the journeys of Abraham and Sarah. Comfortable in retirement, they are called to a place that is unknown to them. Even the route is uncertain. All they have are words of guidance from a mysterious and adventurous God: "Go from your country and your kindred and your father's house to the land that I will show you" (Gen. 12:1). The author of Hebrews expresses their story in light of his own experience as a follower of Jesus: "By faith Abraham obeyed when he was called to set out for a place that he was to receive as an inheritance; and he set out, not knowing where he was going" (Heb. 11:8).

When a group of pastors shared the story of Sarah and Abraham in a contemplative prayer, using the practice of *lectio divina*, a veteran of more than twenty years in ministry responded to the exercise, "This is my story. In a few months I'm retiring and my husband and I are still uncertain about what our retirement life will look like. I'm going on faith, like Sarah; but I wish I could have had the chance to talk with Sarah to get her side of the story. How did she feel when God called them to leave their familiar lifestyle and home? What did she miss most? Was she following Abraham or were they equals in the journey? This small town has become our home, and though we've just purchased a new house in a town nearby, it isn't home yet."

Reading the story of Sarah and Abraham, one assumes that the call of God is chronologically telescoped in the biblical narrative. What took months in real life is described as the fruit of just one holy encounter. Yet God's call to Abraham and Sarah, like God's call to many persons who eventually enter ministry, was likely experienced as hints and inclinations, inspirations and conversations, before the dramatic moment in which Sarah and Abraham said yes to the promise of wilderness adventure. You can imagine them saying to one another, "What have we gotten ourselves into?" as they encounter mishaps and false trails along the way. But despite the mishaps and the uncertainty of their future, they have faith that God is luring them forward by God's presence and promise.

Years ago, when Bruce was a university chaplain at Georgetown University, an insightful undergraduate student reminded a group of anxious first-year students that "God goes to Georgetown, too!" Whether it is the first week of college or the first week of retirement, God is with us. Although our life rituals will change, God's fidelity and care is steadfast. The same God who invited us to embrace the future as young pastors is now inviting us to embark on the new adventure of retirement.

As pastors look at the wilderness adventure of retirement, they can move ahead, like Sarah and Abraham, with the faith that God's call is as lively in retirement as it was in seminary, their first congregation, and at midcareer. The omnipresent and omni-active God has a vision for every stage of life and provides all of us with guidance and companionship in every situation, even the most perplexing. A pastor's calling in this time of spiritual and vocational transition is often simply to pause long enough, amid making plans and packing boxes, to experience God's vision and guidance reassuring and urging her or him to the next step of the adventure. The spiritual practices of pausing and opening to God's presence through prayer and meditation throughout the previous seasons of ministry will prepare a pastor for the meditative pauses necessary to find her or his path through preparation for retirement and into the first steps on the journey beyond full-time congregational ministry.

The adventures of Abraham and Sarah remind us that often life's most important journeys occur in stages (Gen. 12:9). Even if a clearly defined retirement date or departure from the parsonage has been established, healthy preparation for retirement involves intentional acts of faithfulness and stewardship related to finances, housing, friendships, avocations, relationships, and professional duties. Each act of faithful preparation involves both letting go and moving forward. If a person's thoughts center on present responsibilities alone, she or he will never have time to embrace the new adventure toward which God calls her or him.

In the months, and even years, leading up to their retirement, pastors are challenged to become intentional about letting go of certain duties and commitments and embracing new possibilities for personal and professional growth. The word *decision* means "cutting off" certain possible futures, and the intentional pastor recognizes her or his finitude and the finitude of her or his pastoral work. Not every pastoral task can be completed; nor can a person achieve all of his or her goals in life. If a pastor is to have adequate time for retirement preparation—including spiritual reflection, shared conversations, logistical and financial issues, and conversations with retired pastors—she or he must begin to let go of certain nonessential pastoral activities and wean her- or himself from the tyranny of the urgent. As one pastor related, "When I began to think about retirement, I knew I had to balance faithfulness to the church with fidelity to my future vocation and my spouse. I mapped out all of my pastoral duties over the next six months, circled all of the essential ones, and, after a conversation with my spiritual director and vestry chair, began to withdraw from programs that could get along without me." Another pastor saw the time limitation as a gift for himself and the congregation, "Like Jesus, I had to trust that God would be at work in my congregation after I left and that some tasks would have to wait until the next pastor arrived. My calling was simply to be faithful now and in the next few months."

In many ways, pastors prepare best for their retirement by practicing mindful and reflective ministry throughout their ministerial careers. Indeed, one of the goals of this text is to remind pastors that a commitment to self-awareness, openness to God's leading, and professional self-care are at the heart of vital and healthy ministry at every stage of life. For decades prior to retirement, vital and healthy pastors have ideally made decisions that honor their many callings—family, sabbath, health, recreation, spiritual formation, financial stability, friendships, and professional excellence. All of these decisions have involved letting go of certain attractive possibilities in order to embrace even more life-fulfilling possibilities for the present and future. Preparing for retirement is no different than any other short- and long-term planning and decision making throughout ministry—a person can do many things well but must choose *not* to do certain things in order to be faithful to her or his calling in its many dimensions. One pastor noted, "Once I realized that the Christian education committee could do without me, I discovered that I could let go of many activities I once thought were necessary. I said my goodbyes after making sure that the leadership was well-prepared and devoted several hours a week to planning the future with my wife, creating files for my successor, and tying up loose interpersonal ends."

Abraham and Sarah went by stages. They didn't have to arrive all at once at their promised destination. In the course of their journey, Abraham and Sarah set up altars wherever they stopped. These altars were practices of self-awareness and hope that reminded them that God was with them in the wilderness. Gordon Forbes sought out a spiritual director to help him discern God's presence in the first five years beyond retirement. Other pastors may choose to immerse themselves in prayer or in reading books on the spirituality of aging and retirement. While not all pastors will choose to embody the stage of solitary "forest dwelling," characteristic of the Hindu ideal of retirement, an intentional approach to aging and retirement calls pastors in the winter of their ministry to an inner journey that will be reflected in their own unique outer vocation in the retirement years. In turning toward contemplative practices appropriate to her or his personality type, a person discovers a richness of experience that will flow forth in new possibilities for faithfulness in retirement.

Abram and *Sarai* were called to make a vision quest in the course of which they experienced disorientation and uncertainty before they received the blessings of new names, *Abraham* and *Sarah*. Like Native American young adults on their vision quests, Abraham and Sarah grew in wisdom and stature and revised the maps of their world. Their new names reflected their new vocations and duties to bless the earth. For them and for us, such a journey into the wilderness is an act faith and hope. As one pastor affirmed, "I'd forgotten to be anything else but a pastor after forty years of preaching, visiting, and teaching. Now that I'm seldom addressed as 'Reverend' anymore, I'm having fun deciding what name I should go by. Right now, I'm playing with calling myself 'wisdom giver' or 'poet' or 'bike rider.'" When asked to describe the new name she would adopt following retirement, another pastor used words such as "crone," "gardener of the soul," "Sophia sage," and "grandma."

As you listen to God's presence in your life today, what new names is God calling you to embrace? While you will always have a vocation, indeed, many vocations in the years ahead, one of which is minister of the gospel, what other vocations is God calling you toward in the next stage of your journey? What name is God calling you to go by? In the sections ahead, we will reflect upon a few of the tasks of ministerial retirement, each of which clears the way for the next steps on the holy adventure that is God's calling in your life—forgiveness and healing, celebration, finishing well in ministry, transformed relationships, and new images of the future.

Forgiveness and Healing

Psychiatrist and author M. Scott Peck began *The Road Less Traveled* with the words, "Life is difficult."[8] Even the happiest childhood and most fulfilling of ministries contain painful moments that leave wounds that shape the rest of our lives. Take a moment to look back on your own ministry or the ministry of your partner or spouse in light of the following questions:

- Where did you or your partner or spouse experience pain or misunderstanding in the quest to be faithful to God in the course of your ministry?
- In what ways did individuals in your congregations purposely or unintentionally hurt you or your partner or spouse?
- How have you or your spouse or partner responded to the pain you have felt in ministry?
- Do you still have memories or relationships that need God's healing touch?

Then, reflecting on your own ministry, think about such questions as:

- Where have you fallen short in your ministry?

- Where do you need to seek the forgiveness of your spouse, partner, or a parishioner?

Sadly, many pastors go to their retirement still harboring animosity at a congregation's behavior decades ago. Others are burdened by regret over sins of omission or pastoral imperfections. Over the years, many pastors we know of, including ourselves, have been hurt in ministry by insensitive unilateral decisions made by institutional or congregational leaders: judicatory officials who failed to submit a ministerial profile to a congregational search committee as we had requested; congregations who did not, or could not, provide adequate compensation; persons diagnosed with character disorders who stirred up controversies; persecution for social or political views; or persons and congregations that fall into the category, "clergy killers." Others have been damaged by sexism, racism, or homophobia. Some have felt the aftershocks of a previous pastor's or senior colleague's sexual misconduct in ways that undeservedly rocked their own ministry. Every pastor has her or his own "trail of tears" and has wondered, at least once in the course of a ministry, whether or not it was all worth it. Often beneath many pastoral smiles, unresolved anger and hurt remain hidden or repressed. Even if one's pain was undeserved, holding onto memories of negative events ultimately imprisons a person in the past and prevents her or him from moving forward with God into the future.

Forgiveness is the key to healing throughout ministry and especially in preparation for retirement. Going on a spiritual vision quest, a contemplative process in which one opens to God's future, requires a person to let go any excess baggage, most especially feelings of alienation, animosity, grievance, or unforgiveness. At the onset of the retirement vision quest, the question is, "Do you want to be healed? Do you want to experience peace and wholeness?"

The United Church of Christ liturgy "Service for Ending an Authorized Ministry" invites both the pastor and the congregation to ask forgiveness for their mistakes as well as to express gratitude for gifts of leadership, a ritual that serves as a prelude to moving on to the next stage in the lives of the congregation and the soon-departing pastor. The affirmation in the liturgy, "I forgive you and accept your gratitude, trusting that our time together and our parting are pleasing to God" is an important step toward embracing the next stages of a pastor's retirement journey.[9]

Forgiveness is an act of grace that opens the door to the future. Freed of the burdens of past injustice, pain, and hurt, we can embark creatively on the next stages of life's adventure. One of the first acts of forgiveness for some pastors involves recognizing and letting go of their anger at those persons, such as judicatory officials and colleagues, who must remind them that appropriate ethical boundaries require them to distance themselves from persons and groups in the congregation that have shaped their daily lives for years. As they go through the various interdependent stages of grief that emerge as they leave a beloved congregation and their life work, many pastors imagine bargaining with the new pastor or the judicatory official to let them remain involved in some aspect of their former congregation's life, such as the theological study group, choir, or shawl ministry. But as one pastor recalls, "Although I wanted to hang on to the best of my congregation, I knew that faithfulness to my calling and love for this church, not some legalism imposed from above, called me to move on to another congregation. Although the first few months seemed like a wilderness with no direction, now I've found my way. My wife and I are happy in a neighboring congregation and are meeting new friends, not as congregational leaders that have to play a specific role, but as faithful Christians fitting into the life a new church."

Forgiveness is not denial or the acceptance of injustice but courageous openness to God's healing presence, which can transform and heal the present moment, the meaning of the past, and imperfect ministerial relationships. It can also enable a person to have realistic expectations of ambiguous institutions so that she or he can welcome the possibilities embedded in a new identity and vocation. Indeed, pastors must allow themselves to feel the pain of congregational insensitivity, as well as the grief inherent in observing proper ministerial boundaries, in order to feel God's healing invitation to the next steps of their journey. As one pastor recalls, "I couldn't move ahead until I left the pain of my last congregation behind. The wise words of my spiritual guide and the conference minister allowed me to recognize the good I had done there, let go of my mistakes, and begin plans for a new kind of ministry. They reminded me that my calling did not end with retirement from a troubled congregation, but would continue in new and creative ways, especially if I allowed myself to imagine God's next vocational dream for my life."

Practicing forgiveness is essential to the spirit of new life. Jesus's words on the cross, "Father, forgive them, for they know no what they do," paved the way for his own resurrection experience. Renewing our minds through forgiveness transforms our vocational pasts and opens us to God's calling for our future.

Celebrating Ministry

In reflecting on his experience of the sacred, John Ames, the protagonist of *Gilead*, recalls that one of his first "pastoral acts"—the baptism of a litter of cats when he was small boy. "Everyone has petted a cat, but to touch one like that, with the pure intention of blessing it, is a very different thing."[10] While Ames notes that anyone can confer a blessing, people expect pastors to bless them. Blessing is at the heart of ministerial practice. By words spoken and deeds enacted at pivotal moments, or tipping points, in people's lives, pastors share, awaken, and mediate to others the fullness of life identified with God's blessing. Like the shaman and medicine persons who came before them, pastors are seen as persons of power and grace who, through various rituals of passage and celebration as well as the quality of their personal spirituality, reveal and transmit the energy of healing, inspiration, guidance, and forgiveness. Like Abraham and Sarah, pastors are "blessed to be a blessing."

Celebration is an essential aspect of the retirement vision quest. Ritual celebrations, even in the context of mourning the end of a ministry, are affirmations that the pastor's life and work have made, and will continue to make, a difference to others, to those she or he loves, and, above all, to God. Celebration involves claiming the many ways that one's vocation as pastor was and is truly God's work in a particular time and place. Pastors in the winter of ministry celebrate their successes but also celebrate themselves. Years ago Kate learned a simple chant from her spiritual director, Isabella Bates of the Shalem Institute for Spiritual Formation in Washington, D.C.: "I thank you, God, for the wonder of my being." This prayerful chant awakens all of us to God's faithfulness, guidance, and love, working through our vocational adventures.

Looking back on your ministry, where can you celebrate "the wonder of your being"? For what are you grateful? Where can you witness to God's transforming power working in your life in a unique and holy way? Like Esther, where did you find yourself inspired and faithful "for just such a time as this"? Our prayer is that you will find time, at minimum, to celebrate your ministry with the chant, "I thank you, God, for the wonder of my ministry," and, at maximum, with an ongoing series of daily rituals that keep the light of God's presence shining brightly in your life.

Looking back appreciatively on the journey of ministry prepares pastors to look forward with hope toward the next steps of the retirement adventure. Over their some twenty or forty years of ministry, pastors have entered persons' lives in ways that they could never have imagined in advance. Some persons are alive today because a pastor helped them through a time of suicidal depression. Other persons found meaning and direction because a pastor took the time to meet them for a cup of coffee each week or confronted them with an alternative vision for their lives when they were stuck in a rut. Still other congregants entered the ordained ministry because they heard God's call through their pastor's words to them or were inspired by her or his ministerial fidelity and insight. The wheel of pastoral mentoring and inspiration continues to turn.

Think back for a moment: whose faithfulness and care enabled you to see yourself as a pastor? One pastor who had spent two decades saying no to seminary because ministry was for men, not women, recalls with gratitude the time when a male minister not only told her that he believed she could be a pastor but took the day off to accompany her to Andover-Newton Theological School to help her register for seminary. Another pastor recalls the weekly conversations with a seminary professor who helped him imagine God in new ways when, during his first year in seminary, his faith in archaic images of God was seriously challenged.

Every pastor needs a "George Bailey" experience. The protagonist of the movie *It's a Wonderful Life,* George Bailey had a mystical experience in which he saw the faces of those around him whose lives had been transformed through his attempts to be faithful to his calling. Like George Bailey, pastors in the winter of their ministry need to take account—to say thank you and to receive thanks—as they celebrate God's working through their lives to bring wholeness to others, Shalom. Although God's grace is always inspiring and energizing each of us, God's grace does not minimize your own achievements. God worked through you—*your* lives, *your* words, and *your* love—to bring God's healing touch or resurrection spirit to another person at a pivotal time in his or her life. Like Esther, God prepared *you* through a lifetime of responses to God's call to be God's agent for "such a time as this." As one pastor recalls after forty years of ministry, "Every so often, someone calls me up to say thank you for the difference I made in their lives. Sometimes the most unlikely persons express their gratitude. A middle-aged businessman recently stopped by to share a story about how twenty years ago the acceptance he felt at the youth group I led changed his life. I was touched that he gratefully remembered our retreats, toasting s'mores at the campfire, teen dances, and service projects. Often when I'm wondering if my ministry made any difference, God sends someone to remind me that even the simplest acts can change a life."

At various times of a pastor's journey, but especially during the period before or after retirement, we suggest that a pastor take a pilgrimage of celebration. While a pastor can't immediately go back to visit the congregation from which he or she has just retired, a pastor can take a pilgrimage back through time to visit with those he or she once served. The two of us rejoiced when we returned to Saguaro Christian Church in Tucson, Arizona, where we had been ordained, and met the children of teens who were part of our youth group nearly thirty years before. Bruce felt a sense of gratitude for his interim ministry at Downsville Christian Church, near Hagerstown, Maryland, when six of his "baptizands" greeted him in the parking lot of a nearby congregation where he was to give the guest sermon.

The Jewish wisdom saying *tikkun olam* affirms that when you save one soul, you save the world. The logic of this affirmation is simple: given that the world cannot be saved until every soul discovers her or his true identity, the healing of one soul heals the whole world. As you look at your ministry in light of God's graceful movements in your life, how many times over the years did you bring wholeness or rescue a lost sheep in the wilderness? Where has God inspired you, through the synchronous events of life, to be God's partner in healing the world by being part of a person's spiritual transformation? Celebrate these partnerships and synchronicities!

As pastors prepare for retirement, they can naturally celebrate and let go of the simple acts of faithful ministry that they have performed year after year and day after day. They may not think of them as special, but these moments have been life transforming for themselves and others. As another pastor notes, "After twenty years at First Church, I've discovered something interesting. The people really have listened to my sermons. While I didn't intend for them to adopt my theological position, I hear my phrases and ideas coming back to me in conversations and class discussions. It's a humbling but a joyful experience to recognize that even though

I'm no professor, I've been their theologian all these years." In re-membrance of years of faithful preaching and teaching, you might journal the thoughts that inspired your spiritual leadership or create a collage celebrating the theology that guided your preaching.

Celebrating your vocation as a pastor enables you to embrace hope and imagination on your vision quest. You celebrate your gifts in ministry and graces mediated to others, giving thanks for God's presence in a humble and imperfect ministry. But celebration is also corporate; it involves claiming the gifts you have received in the course of your ministerial journey.

One pastor notes that what sustained him most in ministry were the simple caring relationships among the elder adults in his congregation. "Many of them are dead now. But I can see the faces of dozens of elder adults with whom I've visited over the years. More often than not, I left my visits having experienced the blessing of their faithfulness and love for me, first as a young pastor, and now as a seasoned pastor in my sixties." Another pas-tor posts photographs of his congregations proudly on the wall of his study. "Those churches are my harvest, but I am their harvest as well. Living with them through the years made me what I am today. In those six churches, filled with ordinary people, I grew to be a pastor and discovered the meaning of faith. I'm grateful for their trust in me and their willingness to place their spiritual lives in my care."

As they look back on their ministries, most pastors celebrate the simple and ordinary acts of ministry—the opportunity to be their congregation's "rabbi," to study and preach, and to enter persons' lives in times of vulnerability. No idealists about the church and its members, these pastors have firsthand experience of congregational conflict and ineptitude, difficult parishioners, and unfulfilled per-sonal and professional dreams. But their pastoral imagination has enabled them to celebrate the joy of divine inspiration and recon-ciliation in the baptizing of infants, discussing issues of faith with teenagers, playing games with children, and rejoicing in meaningful worship services. Looking back on decades of ministry, they joyfully affirm in their own words the sentiments of one United Methodist pastor, "Despite all the challenges of ministry, this is my calling and for this calling I was made." In celebrating the past, they can look hopefully toward their future retirement with the words of Dag Hammarskjold:

> Night is drawing nigh—
> For all that has been—Thanks!
> For all that shall be—Yes![11]

Finishing Well in Ministry

While some pastors feel a sense of loss of power and become lame ducks as soon as they announce their retirement, others recognize a higher goal of integration and celebration as they are called to live by the maxim, "leading while you're leaving." A pastor planning to retire is still pastor of the congregation and not a mere figurehead. She or he will in fact always be a pastor even in retirement, although the venue of ministry will change. The times are too crucial in the church today for retiring pastors to recede into the background, fulfilling their roles without purpose or vitality. In the months prior to retirement, pastors are called to let their light shine rather than fade away. As they ponder their final months in full-time congregational ministry, pastors have two complementary, albeit different, tasks in finishing well—they must spiritually and professionally prepare for retirement and at the same time minister with vision and vigor till their final day.

In an earlier section, we stressed the importance of pastors working with their spouses and partners as well as with congregational leaders in order to withdraw gradually from certain nonessential ministerial activities and prepare themselves and their community for the transition to retirement. Retired pastors say "less is more" when it comes to the final months in ministry—less involvement in the details of building upkeep and supervision of staff; fewer but more meaningful visits to shut-ins; gradual turning over issues of evangelism, new member assimilation, and leadership development to colleagues in ministry and lay leaders; letting others take the lead in strategic planning and congregational visioning. The long-term practice of self-differentiation in ministry pays off at such times. Both you and your congregants will be grateful. Finishing well in ministry involves the interplay of withdrawal and presence, much like planning for a sabbatical leave. As a pastor begins to imagine the last year in full-time ministry, he or she should call together congregational leaders as well as outside professional consultants, such as judicatory officials, to discern the focus and flow of the final months or year.

In every season of ministry, God inspires us with new and creative ideas, and therefore preretirement presents another important time for a person to grow and mature in ministry and congregational life. Ministers may choose to focus in their sermons on themes such as: "What I've learned in ministry," "Things I've never preached about," or "The last sermon series." They may also address issues such as the nature of boundary issues, grief, transition, and gratitude, carefully using her or his own preretirement and retirement passage as a laboratory for the congregation to face its upcoming loss, transition, grief, and celebration in a healthy manner. A pastor's ongoing commitment to spiritual, personal, and professional growth throughout all the seasons of ministry helps churches to see their own transitional period as passages to be creatively embraced and full of celebration and growth.

While a pastor's public witness to growth during retirement preparation is important, the private witness is equally important. It invites pastors to see their vocation as congregational spiritual leaders in new ways. While the months prior to retirement should not normally be occasions of initiating long-range planning, beginning a capital campaign, or starting a new type of worship service, much can still be done at an interpersonal leadership level—a pastor may take time to bless, forgive, and accept the blessing of particular persons within his or her congregation. With nothing to lose, a pastor may speak with a prophetic voice about social justice issues near and dear to her or his heart. He or she may also choose to build bridges of reconciliation with a difficult parishioner or speak words of appreciation and encouragement to those who have been most supportive or inspiring in his or her ministry. In all these encounters, the pastor's goal is personal and corporate healing and wholeness, modeling for the congregation how to discover creative ways to embrace and transform relationships in the way of Jesus. In so doing, he or she enables the congregation to experience the graceful hospitality of the One who welcomed and transformed persons in every station of life.

As he or she says goodbye, the pastor's ultimate goal is to remind the congregation that God is faithful and present through all the changes of life and that nothing—not even the departure of a beloved pastor—can separate them from the love of God. In God's great abundance, God will inspire new leaders from among the congregation who will carry on in their own unique and faithful way the good work that they shared with the retiring pastor. Holy leave-takings inspire congregations to claim their own resources for healing, wholeness, and transformation in light of God's vision of its future.

Transforming Ministerial Relationships

Throughout this book, we have stressed the importance of healthy relationships within and beyond the congregation. Vital and fruitful ministry is nourished by a strong commitment to maintaining relationships with colleagues and friends outside the congregation. Yet, because of the interdependent nature of all relationships, all of these are transformed, including the pastor's relationship to her or his family, when the church is no longer the center of one's personal or professional life. If both the pastor and his or her spouse or partner choose to retire within the same period of time, they will have to navigate with particular care how to spend the extra time they may have together and apart during the day and in the evening hours. New familial behaviors and boundaries will need to be explored intentionally to make the most of the forty to sixty hours that immediately open up each week. Many couples choose to travel or build a new home following retirement. Others explore hobbies and volunteer work that they can do both individually and together as a couple. One couple noted that they now have time to read the *New York Times* on Sunday mornings and spend time gardening on Sunday afternoons. "After church, we simply go home and have lunch while we listen to *A Prairie Home Companion*. After forty years of busy Sundays, this is heaven! The Sabbath is finally a sabbath for the two of us." One pastor jokes, "While I don't golf on Sunday morning, my wife and I have found golf to be our new love, along with spending time with our grandchildren."

As they prepare for retirement, couples need to consider each person's unique personality needs. For example, couples who embody the introvert-extrovert polarity find they need to plan activities that bridge differences and enable them to meet in the middle, as well as individual activities that nurture their unique personalities. By embracing each other's uniqueness, couples grow in wisdom and stature and continue the process of individuation, or the spiritual maturity characteristic of life's winter.

After several months, many retired pastors may choose to return to ministry as interim ministers, stated supply ministers, or guest preachers, because these pastors still have "fire in the belly" for congregational leadership, teaching, and preaching. These pastors will continue to practice ministry in other congregations but will often enjoy ministry without the same level of intense personal attachment, community engagement, energy expenditure, and long-term commitment. Some pastors report that they can be free to preach and lead for the sheer joy of it. Fulfilling their ongoing vocation as God's partners in congregational transformation and healing but in more flexible and short-term ways can be renewing and fun. As he looks toward retirement, the senior pastor of a multiple-staff congregation looks forward to several years of interim ministry: "My spouse and I want to travel to interesting places and do interesting work. I realize that interim pastors with multiple-staff experience are in great demand and I want to respond to that need. I've taken interim ministry training and anticipate circulating my profile six months after my retirement. I need the stimulation. I can imagine doing interims in places like Tucson, Boulder, Santa Fe, Hawaii, and California." In this same spirit, a retired naval chaplain, now serving as an interim pastor, has enrolled in a part-time Clinical Pastoral Education program not only to enhance his ministerial skills, but also to volunteer with the Red Cross in crisis response.

A few months following retirement, another pastor made it known that she would enjoy supply preaching and retreat leadership. "I preach once or twice every month and lead several spiritual life retreats a year. It keeps me intellectually lively and also provides extra income for vacations." These pastors have learned the Zen of retirement— that is, commitment to ministerial excellence for its own sake without the need to "get ahead" in ministry or to see one's whole life as connected with the church. Their spiritual detachment may actually be an asset in creative congregational leadership.

Because practicing appropriate boundaries with former congregations is important, many pastors still find sustenance through ongoing professional relationships with colleagues. As one pastor notes, "I made it through the first year because I made it a point to stay in touch with colleagues. I regularly went to the ministerium and joined an informal group of retired pastors that met monthly in the area. We shared stories, read books together, and drank gallons of coffee. I found that some of the younger pastors came to me for advice, and that meant a lot to me. I still had something to give." Other pastors immerse themselves in the resources of the local seminary, attending lectures, studying in the library, and offering their services as mentors to seminarians or new pastors. Still others now have time to become active volunteers in soup kitchens, the local council of churches, or symphonies and other civic groups. Without the pressure of full-time ministry, they can share more freely their professional skills—public speaking, volunteer coordination and recruitment, outreach, teaching—in a context where they can still make a difference, whether as a tutor, library or museum volunteer, teacher's aide, or community college teacher.

Embracing a New Identity

According to legend, Celtic spiritual guides often set out on the high seas, traveling in rudderless boats called "coracles." Trusting God to guide their skiffs, they set sail for their unknown place of resurrection, the contemplative environment in which they would find their spiritual home. While today's pastors travel with the rudder of intentionality and collegial support, the destination of the retirement vision quest, whether it involves a new home or a deepening sense of God's presence in a familiar setting, is always a journey toward the unknown. The quest is fraught with risks that are only ameliorated with self-knowledge and an actively embraced sense of appreciation of the limits of aging.

As he or she contemplates the retirement vision quest, virtually every pastor has moments in which she or he asks, "Who will I be once I am no longer a pastor? Will I go forth with energy and inspiration or just fade away? How will I describe myself when I am no longer a pastor?" Pastors who have established close friendships and interests beyond ministry have an easier time responding positively to these questions.

Pastoral vision quests are, first of all, journeys of the imagination. Freed from the constraints of full-time responsibilities, pastors considering retirement are called to imagine new spiritual possibilities. Retirement is no time for stagnation. Echoing the Pentecost proclamation from Acts 2: "Your young men [and women] shall see visions, and your old men [and women] shall dream dreams," God is still speaking and doing a new thing in retirement. Like the aged Simeon and Anna in Luke's Gospel who recognized the baby Jesus in the temple, pastors in the winter of ministry are challenged to seek and to recognize the surprising things God is doing in their lives today. With the possibility of many years of good health ahead of them, pastors in their sixties can let their imaginations roam in new directions as God's partners in transforming the world.

Winter has a spirituality of its own, which is contemplative in nature. Simplicity of life is also one of the callings of winter in ministry. As pastors let go of previous ways they encountered God in the days they served God as pastors, they now can discover God's new calling to be wisdom givers. Gordon Forbes sought out the counsel of an experienced spiritual guide and made a commitment to the daily practice of *lectio divina,* reading Scripture contemplatively in companionship with his wife. Clayton Gooden, the senior pastor of the congregation in which Kate served as both an intern and a youth pastor, found joy and meaning as a painter, writer, and artist following retirement. Still another pastor, Julia, sees her study at home as a new holy place. "I look out the windows, pondering the beauty as I read theological and spiritual classics I didn't have time to read when I was a full-time pastor. Now I can focus on my own spiritual growth, my own sense of God's presence, rather than focusing primarily on the spiritual well-being of others. Who knows? As God becomes more real to me, I may become a more effective messenger of God in retirement than I was when I was a full-time pastor."

With retirement, some pastors explore the ultimate horizons of life. While they anticipate many years of creativity and health, pastors may experience the retirement vision quest as the first of many opportunities to "let go" into God's care. Death may be decades away, and they can imaginatively reflect upon a journey from young elder to middle elder and, eventually, to old elder. Integrity in aging is grounded in the trust that our lives have truly mattered and that when we can no longer care for ourselves, God will remain trustworthy. For many this may mean imaging a new form of interdependence—once they saw themselves as congregational and community shapers; now they are challenged to imagine what it might mean to be vulnerable, trusting their children and friends to support them when their own energy is depleted. Someday they may be called to embrace the role reversal of accepting the pastoral care of a minister in her or his first congregational call or navigating the challenges of midcareer ministry. Knowing that nothing in all creation, neither life nor death, nor sickness, nor disability, can separate us from the love of God, pastors in the winter of ministry can embrace their vulnerability in new ways. God is present through every season of life and ministry, and the harvest of winter, the harvest of one's commitments and faithfulness, is one's gift to generations to come.

Harvesting Wisdom

When many pastors retire, they fear loneliness, stagnation, and loss of identity. But God is alive and still moving in their lives and in the world As the new creed from the United Church of Canada affirms, "We are not alone; we live in God's world." In affirming the spirit of the creed, "We believe in God: who has created and is creating. . . . to reconcile and make new, who works in us and others by the Spirit. We trust in God," pastors will find their retirement fruitful and enriching.

Lancaster Theological Seminary's Harvesting Wisdom program was inspired by the vision of a faithful and dynamic God, constantly doing new things in pastors' lives and in congregations, throughout all the seasons of ministry, including retirement and preretirement. The program was initiated in 2006 as a way of nurturing wholeness for pastors as they prepare for retirement or as they take the first steps beyond full-time ministry. For many years, Bruce had heard stories told by experienced pastors, younger associates, and active laypersons about the difficulties many pastors face as they prepare for retirement. He found that too many pastors spend their last years in ministry simply waiting to retire, worn down by a sense of failure, fatigue, and frustration. Convinced that healing, wholeness, and new life are possible at every stage of ministry, Bruce gathered a focus group of pastors who had recently retired or who were at retirement age to reflect on the spiritual, emotional, relational, and vocational issues confronting pastors considering retirement. Shortly thereafter, Bruce recruited David Rich, a retired Presbyterian minister with significant experience in leading pre-retirement groups for clergy, and Peter Schmiechen, a United Church of Christ minister and recently retired president of Lancaster Theological Seminary, to help lead colleague groups of preretirement and recently retired ministers.

As with all of Lancaster Theological Seminary's ministerial excellence programs, Harvesting Wisdom is guided by the apostle Paul's affirmation that God will complete the good work God has begun in our lives with the promise of a harvest of righteousness. David Rich adds his own version of Paul's affirmation, "It is not as important how you start as how you finish." The goal of Harvesting Wisdom is to finish well in full-time ministry, celebrating achievements, practicing forgiveness, and discerning a vision for the first years following retirement.

Grounded in a positive vision of growth beyond retirement, the expressed purpose of Harvesting Wisdom is to provide an opportunity for pastors to: (1) understand the nature of transitions and the importance of achieving a healthy and positive conclusion of their ministry with their current congregation; (2) review and reflect on their years in ministry, balancing gratitude and appreciation with grief, forgiveness, and letting go; (3) identify how they can do their best work in ministry in their final months or years so that they can finish with purpose, vitality, and creativity; and (4) develop a plan with the congregation so that they creatively and effectively work together in the transition toward retirement.

As in all clergy groups, financial issues sometimes emerge in the seminar, but the primary focus is spiritual, vocational, and relational. Participants are initially invited to look back at times of fulfillment and emptiness in order to affirm what they have learned over the years about themselves, to embrace their losses, and celebrate their accomplishments. Then as part of this process of mindful and self-aware ministry, they are asked to reflect on their current spiritual and physical health, level of energy, use of time, and sense of calling. Turning toward the future, they are challenged to explore where they would like to focus in their final months or years of ministry and to identify their dreams for their congregation as they prepare to retire. Participants are asked what they would like to achieve and what they need to jettison in order to finish with vitality and purpose. In the process of reflecting on their vision for the future, participants are asked to make a transition plan for themselves and the congregation that may include issues of communication about one's retirement, setting boundaries for oneself and others, ways to express gratitude and say goodbye, areas of healing and wholeness in congregational relationships, practical issues of helping the congregation understand the search process, and preparing information and files for the next pastor. As one pastor noted, "The seminar enabled me to gain perspective on where I was, what I was feeling, and what I should expect in the future. I felt less panicked as I imagined retiring."[12]

In the course of their group sharing, pastors discover that they are not alone in their feelings of uncertainty, anticipatory grief, and excitement. As one reflected, "My husband and I thought we were the only ones who were ambivalent about retirement. Now I know that most every pastor feels the way I do. As a result of our group experiences, the secret's out—I have a whole new group of friends with whom I can be honest about how I feel without worrying about being judged."

The name "harvesting wisdom" reveals the ultimate goal as well as the process of this seminar. The approach of the program assumes that retired ministers can choose to be wisdom givers, sharing their experience and insights with new generations of pastors. God's vision for our lives is constant and intimate, dynamically changing as we change, providing new possibilities and the energy to pursue them at every stage of life. In an interdependent world, retired pastors still have a vocation of providing guidance, perspective, and wisdom that can be embraced by their denominations. Indeed, a truly multigenerational church honors and welcomes the visions of wise women and men as it explores new frontiers of faithfulness and service.

Spiritual Practices for Winter in Ministry

The following exercises and spiritual practices can help you with visioning and letting go, the tasks of this season of ministry.

Writing Your Spiritual Autobiography

The combined insights of Frederick Buechner and Parker Palmer create a type of literary call and response with their two autobiographical proclamations: "Listen to your life" and "Let your life speak." While it is always helpful to make narrative notations in every time of transition and transformation, writing a spiritual autobiography when one is considering retirement or has recently retired is a particularly powerful tool for learning about your life's various patterns and movements. The mere attempt to write a spiritual autobiography during each major life transition and passage is grounded in the grand affirmation, "Your life matters," and that in the course of your journey, you have made countless choices that have shaped your personal adventure and the lives of others. Writing a spiritual autobiography reminds you that, whether or not your life is well-known to others, your life is a heroic testimony to faith and perseverance in which you have faced obstacles, confronted fears, grown through crises, and fulfilled your vocation, imperfectly but faithfully, to be sure.[13]

Those who attempt a spiritual autobiography discover the unique value and impact of their apparently unimportant and unnoticed lives. While there are many books on spiritual autobiography and writing, there is no one way of telling your story. Perhaps, the call and response of listening to your life and letting your life speak are a good place to begin as you reflect on such experiences as:

- The home you grew up in, both architecturally and emotionally
- Your best friends in childhood
- The moment God became more than a word to you
- When you fell in love for the first time
- The way you felt on your wedding day or when your children were born
- Your discovery that God has called you to ministry
- Life in seminary
- Your first congregation
- Major personal disappointments, losses, or tragedies
- Times of celebration in your ministry and personal life
- The primary lessons you have learned over the years
- How your image of God has changed over the years
- Central theological affirmations that have guided your life
- Your dreams for the years ahead

The goal of writing your spiritual autobiography is, first of all, self-awareness, self-affirmation, and healing. As Erik Erikson notes, aging can bring despair but it can also be a time of integrity, of the healthy integration of the many aspects of your life.[14] While writing a spiritual autobiography is at first a solitary, contemplative venture designed to enhance your own sense of wholeness and holiness, it is also a great gift to your children and grandchildren, colleagues and companions, whose own journeys have been and will be enriched by knowing you and experiencing, through reading your reflections, their own lives and the lives of beloved others.

Spiritual Obituary

Writing your own obituary is another exercise that can deepen your self-awareness and help set your compass in retirement. While most published obituaries simply state the facts of a person's life in a dry fashion, a spiritual obituary enables the writer to look back upon her or his life and to look ahead toward the future in way that enables the writer to see the interplay of the many values that shaped her or his life. While the writer is not obligated to assume how he or she shall die, a spiritual obituary is a testimony to the values by which the person lived. The following questions can help you think about God's movements in the course of your professional and personal journey and generate a page or two of written responses:

- What values have motivated your life?
- What is your image of God and how has it shaped your spiritual journey?
- What was your most heroic moment?
- What do you most want to celebrate in your life?
- What do you most want to celebrate in your ministry?
- Whom have you loved in the course of your life?
- What are your favorite hobbies and pastimes?
- What key phrases, scriptures, or aphorisms sum up your life?
- What do you plan to do in the remaining years of your life?
- What value or counsel do you leave to the next generation?
- What causes have you devoted your life to?

A complementary exercise to writing a spiritual obituary would be creating a brief epitaph for your tombstone. What might sum up your life, either philosophically or humorously? A tombstone in a historic cemetery in northern Virginia announces, "Dust to dust and ashes to ashes were never said of the soul." Erma Bombeck joked about putting the words "I told you I was sick" on her tombstone. A dentist's tombstone reads, "Dr. Smith is filling his final cavity." Even humor can reveal our values and enable us to look at our lives from a larger perspective, reminding us that one of the gifts of aging and retirement is a sense of life's spaciousness and grandeur within which the moment by moment events of our lives find a home.

Gratitude

Thanksgiving is the cornerstone of a well-lived life. We can move ahead to an unknown future with confidence precisely because we have experienced moments of grace and gratitude in the course of our lives. As you look over your life's journey, for what relationships and events are you most thankful? In your current life, what are the grace notes and joys for which you are thankful? For what persons in your life do you feel most grateful? For what opportunities are you most thankful? For what "failures" are you most thankful?

Take a moment to write a prayer that expresses your gratitude for all of life's gifts. You might choose to sing personally or make an adaptation of a hymn, such as "Now Thank We All Our God," "God of Change and Glory," or "We Gather Together," on a regular basis to express your sense of gratitude for God's presence in your life's adventure and ministerial career. You might even choose to write your own song, poem, or short story to express your gratitude to God and those whose love graced your life.

Gratitude is experienced not only in our relationship with God but in our willingness to thank all of those who have mediated God's presence to us in the course of our lives. Take time to write a letter or e-mail expressing your gratitude to those who have been pivotal in your life, if they are still alive. You may still write a note to a mentor or friend who is no longer living. If he or she has a spouse, partner, or child still living, you might send a note of remembrance and gratitude to that person.

Forgiveness

As you reflect appreciatively on the highest and best moments of your life, you are also invited to remember—and experience—moments of pain and disappointment. In the course of a ministerial adventure, at one time or another, most pastors have felt misunderstood, attacked, neglected, treated unjustly, or professionally abused. You bear the scars of unhealed wounds that shape your current experiences of ministry. These same wounds will shape your attitude toward the church during your retirement. While some wounds are so painful that they require the companionship of a counselor or spiritual guide, we suggest the following imaginative prayer as a way of placing your wounds in God's care:

- Take a few moments simply to be still in God's presence, breathing in God's generous companionship and love, inhaling gently and slowly.
- In the quiet of God's companionship, grounded in each breath, take a moment to remember a painful moment in ministry. Visualize the moment, event, or encounter.
- Reexperience the event and your response to it. How did you feel? In what ways were you hurt?
- How has that pain shaped your ministry? Is it still a burden?
- In the quiet of your meditation, take time again to breathe gently, noticing how your body is reacting to your remembrance.
- As you remember that event, imagine that Jesus or another healing companion is with you. Experience her or his protective presence. In her or his presence, you know that you are safe and secure.
- Visualize yourself sharing your feelings about the event and pain with Jesus or another healing figure. How does the healing figure or Jesus respond? How does the healing figure address those who have hurt you?
- Now, take a moment to place your burden in the hands of Jesus or your healing figure. Along with the emotional pain, notice any physical sensations and let go of the pain, knowing that it need no longer burden you.
- Like the man Jesus encountered at the pool of Siloam, how do you respond to Jesus's question, "Do you want to be healed" of the burdens of the past (John 9:1-7)?

- Experience God's love and grace flowing in and through your life. Take a moment to be present with the healing, loving God.

You may also use a similar exercise to remember God's forgiving presence as you reflect on your own ministerial mistakes and shortcomings.

Visioning Your Future

In this imaginative prayer, visualize yourself on a path toward a place of beauty and fulfillment, the place where you most expect to experience wholeness.

- What does the path look like? Visualize your environment. Is anyone traveling with you? If so, take a moment to visualize your companions on the journey.
- As your journey toward your place of beauty and fulfillment progresses, visualize what that place would look like and what you will want to do there.
- As you walk, visualize yourself being approached by Jesus or another holy figure, who catches up with you and, then, walks with you. How do you feel when you experience this holy one walking beside you?
- Then experience Jesus, or this other holy figure, asking you a few questions: "What beauty do you want to experience? What dreams do you want to fulfill? What legacy do you want to leave?" As you walk along, you may share your dreams of the future with Jesus or this other holy one. Notice how you feel in the course of the conversation.
- When you find yourself at the outskirts of your place of wholeness and peace, notice what the place looks like. Is anyone waiting for you there or do you remain alone with the holy one?

- As you experience the beauty of this place of earthly wholeness, imagine Jesus, or the holy figure, asking you these questions, "How would like to spend your first day of retirement? What activities would you like to do? Where do you want to go? Whom would you like to see?" Take time to share your vision with your holy companion.
- As you prepare to say goodbye, Jesus, or the holy one, gives you a word of counsel: "Today, it is right and good for you to live by your future vision! Today, why don't you do one of the activities that you've planned for your first day of joyful retirement?" By the grace of God your future can begin now!

You can live into future visions by embodying one aspect of your future vision each and every day. Life and time is transformed and made whole as we actively imagine and engage in our hopeful future right now.

Covenant of Spiritual Transformation for Winter in Ministry

As you look toward retirement and beyond, take time to visualize your future and outline your personal covenant of transformation for the future, and begin it now. Remember that God is constantly calling us forward in our lives—as God called Sarah and Abraham—to exciting new adventures and journeys in retirement. While you may articulate a carefully crafted and detailed vision of the future, you may also choose to make covenants as simple as these:

- I covenant to remain active in retirement as I open myself to new visions and dreams for the future.
- I covenant to reach out to make new friends and explore new behaviors and practices in retirement.

- I covenant to let go of the past so that I can more ably share my gifts with pastors who are in the midst of their ministerial adventures.

⟪ 6 ⟫

A Harvest of Righteousness

The story is told of a night long ago when the stars began to fall from the sky. The villagers, surprised by the stars streaking across the sky, panicked and assumed the world was coming to an end. They ran to and fro crying, "The sky is falling, the sky is falling; the world is ending," until one of them remembered the wise ones who lived just outside the village. Frantically, they ran to this older couple in search of an answer. "Look," they shouted, "the stars are falling into the earth. What will happen to us?" The wise ones, who had been observing the changing sky for some time, paused a few moments and asked the villagers to gaze upon the sky one more time. "Look at the sky," they whispered, "look at the stars that are falling. But, now, pause a moment and look again, look this time all the stars that are not falling, but remain shining in the heavens."

When life changes rain down upon us like stars falling from the sky, we can focus on what is faithful and everlasting as well as what is rapidly changing and uncertain, knowing that God embraces both change and stability. Navigating the four seasons of ministry steadily and in a healthy and wise way is the gift of a vision that embraces God's incarnate presence, which abides within a person's truest self as she or he evolves and endures with the changing patterns of her or his life, the church, and a growing experience of God's call. Engaging in apocalyptic thinking is tempting, whether one ponders Loren Mead's "once and future church" or the "once and future minister." But faith calls a person elsewhere. There are few certainties for pastors today—and many dire warnings—as they envisage the future of the church and the vocation of ministry as a whole. Today's pastors, even in relatively quiet rural settings, lead congregations in a time turbulent like permanent whitewater, in which the church on the village green seeks to coexist with the World Wide Web, postmodern relativism, religious pluralism, and hedonistic consumerism.

While pastors may dream of the ministry style reflected by computer-phobic, small-town pastor Father Tim, the protagonist of Jan Karon's Mitford novels, or the bucolic ministry consisting of equal measures of study, sermon preparation, and fly fishing portrayed in the film *A River Runs Through It*, most ministries, rural or urban, are lived out at the speed of twenty-first-century life. Many pastors work nonstop just to keep up with the constant changes in their congregations and communities. Seeking to respond creatively and faithfully to today's challenges, many pastors feel the need not only to constantly update the skills required for responding faithfully to God's call in their ministries, but also to pause to experience God's ever-present guidance in an ever-changing world.

Still, the two of us believe that amid all the transitions and changes that are occurring in culture, church, and ministry, as well as in the lives of pastors who expect to serve the church for two, three, four, or five decades to come, many simple, gentle, and life-affirming practices can serve as polestars for a pastor's healthy, vital, and effective ministry. As we talked with seminarians and pastors who in every season of ministry are achieving healthy excellence in their pastoral vocation as well as in their personal vocations, we discovered that practices supporting ministerial spirituality, excellence, and wholeness in one season of ministry are also essential to healthy and vital ministry in all the other seasons. The varied seasons and their characteristic challenges have a thread of continuity tied to the dynamic yet faithful interplay of divine grace and inspiration and human response and collegial companionship.

Our particular perspective on the seasons of ministry and the nature of pastoral excellence and well-being is shaped by our beliefs in the practices of holistic spiritual formation, family and congregational systems theory, holistic health and wellness, contemporary science, and process theology lived out in the context of mainstream, progressive, and open-spirited traditional congregations. We also believe that pastors, regardless of their theological or liturgical orientation, are nourished and inspired in every season of life by a commitment to embodying practices of self-awareness, wholeness, and professional growth. Certain patterns of professional wholeness and vitality are apparent whether a pastor ascribes to process theology, liberation theology, evangelical theology, or emerging postmodern Christianity. While some theological orientations may de-emphasize the importance of the mind-body-spirit relational interdependence that is key to our perspective, we believe that virtually all healthy and vital pastors are committed to a professional life that integrates theological reflection, continuing education, physical well-being, regular spiritual practices, healthy family life and relationships, and the ability to look at the congregation from a wider perspective than the current congregational crisis.

Ministerial vitality and excellence in every season of life relate to clarity about one's gifts and limitations and a strong sense of God's call, which is not only toward excellence in ordained ministry and spiritual leadership but also toward faithful parenting, physical and spiritual well-being, friendships and relationships, and concern about justice and planetary well-being. We affirm that God calls pastors anew in each moment and over and over again throughout their lifetimes. A pastor's response to God's call forward into newness of life and ministry involves practicing the presence of God in the ordinary tasks of ministry and everyday life as well as in her or his well-visualized and implemented long-term vocational plans. Openness to God's call at all times invites pastors to cultivate the gifts of imagination and flexibility so that amid the anxiety of life and ministry transitions, they can embrace the fullness of God's companionship and divinely given possibilities they had counted on as they set out in ministry.

In all the seasons of ministry and life, God calls pastors to a harvest of righteousness in which they are blessed to be a blessing. In living out the highest aims of ministry, family life, and community and global responsibility, their lives bear fruit that will sustain and transform others long after their formal labors are over. Vital and effective ministry that embraces church, home, and world is the result of nurturing and protecting the seeds of vocational inspiration pastors experienced in the initial springtime call to ministry. A harvest of righteousness is the result of the dynamic interplay of personal commitment and congregational and collegial support during times of crisis, change, and growth. Accordingly, the two of us challenge judicatory commissions on ministry, seminary faculty and administrators, denominational leaders, and colleagues in ministry to promote what we refer to as "a culture of the call" by providing ongoing resources in theological education that promote healthy and embodied ministry throughout a pastor's vocational adventure. We also challenge church leaders to be intentional and creative in responding to the wounds that pastors experience in the course of ministry by providing spiritual and psychological care for them.

A ministerial life characterized by joy, fidelity, service, health, and love is ultimately a matter of call and response—hearing God's call over and over again through various people and places, through all the seasons of life, and always responding to that divine call with a heartfelt "Yes!" Call and response is the dance of divine wisdom and human intentionality in which all of us open ourselves to God's new and creative word for every situation. "Practicing" ministry throughout life's seasons for pastors means responding to God's call by commitments to prayer and devotional reading, continuing theological education, self-differentiation and visionary thinking, healthy intimacy among friends and family, and personal well-being. Through it all, God gently moves, aiming to bring to fullness the good work that God began in your life when you first heard God's call to ministry.

The two of us pray that as you look back on your well-lived professional life in ministry, you and your family can authentically affirm, "Yes, I am glad that God called me to ministry and I am glad I responded to the call! I have followed the path. I have been faithful to my calling and to my callings. I have led and been supported with grace and creativity. By God's grace and the healing companionship of colleagues, friends, and family, I have gathered a harvest of righteousness."

Notes

A Word of Invitation and Thanks

1. To learn about reiki healing touch in the Christian tradition, see Bruce G. Epperly and Katherine Gould Epperly, *Reiki Healing Touch and the Way of Jesus* (Kelowna, British Columbia: Northstone, 2006).
2. For more information on Lancaster Theological Seminary, please consult www.lancasterseminary.edu.
3. For information on Disciples United Community Church, see www.ducc.us.

Chapter 1, The Four Seasons of Ministry

1. For resources on Benedictine spirituality, see Norvene Vest, *Preferring Christ: A Devotional Commentary on the Rule of St. Benedict* (Harrisburg, PA: Morehouse Press, 2004); Norvene Vest, *Friend of the Soul: A Benedictine Spirituality of Work* (Boston: Cowley, 1997); Esther de Waal, *Seeking God: The Way of St. Benedict* (Collegeville, MN: Liturgical Press, 2001).
2. Information on the Shalem Institute for Spiritual Formation can be found at www.shalem.org.
3. For more guidance in the growing interest in practices of faith, see Diana Butler Bass, *Christianity for the Rest of Us: How the Neighborhood Church Is Transforming the Faith* (San Francisco: HarperSanFrancisco, 2006), and Dorothy C. Bass, *Practicing Our Faith: A Way of Life for Searching People* (San Francisco: Jossey-Bass, 1997).

4. Alfred North Whitehead, *Process and Reality*, corr. ed. (New York: Free Press, 1978), 346.
5. For information on centering prayer, see M. Basil Pennington, *The Way Back Home: An Introduction to Centering Prayer* (New York: Paulist Press, 1969) and *Centering Prayer: Renewing an Ancient Christian Prayer Form* (New York: Image Books, 1982).

Chapter 2, Springtime in Ministry: Discernment and Nurture

1. Whitehead, *Process and Reality*, 3.
2. L. Gregory Jones and Kevin R. Armstrong, *Resurrecting Excellence: Shaping Faithful Christian Ministry* (Grand Rapids: Eerdmans, 2006), 152.
3. Abraham Joshua Heschel, *The Sabbath* (New York: Farrar, Straus, and Giroux, 1988).
4. For more on this five-step process of spiritual formation inspired by the work of psychiatrist and spiritual guide Gerald May, see Bruce Epperly and Katherine Epperly, *Feeding the Fire: Avoiding Clergy Burnout* (Cleveland: Pilgrim Press, 2008).
5. Charles R. Foster, Lisa Dahill, Larry Goleman, Barbara Wang Tolentino, *Educating Clergy: Teaching Practices and Pastoral Imagination* (San Francisco: Jossey-Bass, 2005).
6. Ibid., 22.
7. Craig Dykstra, "Pastoral Imagination," *Initiatives in Religion* 9, no. 1 (Spring 2001): 2-3, 15.
8. For more on sabbath, see Tilden Edwards, *Sabbath Time* (New York: Seabury Press, 1992.)
9. An insightful reflection on the benefits of eating locally is found in Barbara Kingsolver's *Animal, Vegetable, Miracle: A Year of Food Life* (New York: Harper Collins, 2007).

Chapter 3, Summertime in Ministry: Adventure and Integrity

1. Richard Lischer, *Open Secrets: A Memoir of Faith and Discovery* (New York: Broadway, 2002), 8-9.
2. Ibid., 49-50.
3. Jackson W. Carroll, *God's Potters: Pastoral Leadership and the Shaping of Congregations* (Grand Rapids: Eerdmans, 2006), 96.
4. Ibid., 69.
5. Reinhold Niebuhr, *Leaves from the Notebook of a Tamed Cynic* (New York: Harper and Row, 1929), 173-74.
6. Charles E. Hummel, *Freedom from the Tyranny of the Urgent* (Downers Grove, IL: InterVarsity Press, 1997).
7. Marcus J. Borg, *Meeting Jesus Again for the First Time: The Historical Jesus and the Heart of Contemporary Faith* (New York: HarperOne, 1995), 32-33.
8. Jackson W. Carroll, *As One with Authority: Reflective Leadership in Ministry* (Louisville: Westminster/John Knox, 1991), 14, 54.
9. Jack Good, *The Dishonest Church* (Bend, OR: Rising Star Press, 2003).
10. For more information on theological and spiritual affirmations, see Bruce G. Epperly, *The Power of Affirmative Faith* (St. Louis: Chalice Press, 2001) and *Holy Adventure: Forty-One Days of Audacious Living* (Nashville: Upper Room, 2008).
11. We recommend the following resources on congregational systems theory: Edwin Friedman, *Generation to Generation: Family Process in Church and Synagogue* (New York: Guilford Press, 1985); Peter L. Steinke, *Congregational Leadership in Anxious Times: Being Calm and Courageous No Matter What* (Herndon, VA: Alban Institute, 2006) and *How Your Church Family Works: Understanding Congregations as Emotional Systems* (Herndon, VA: Alban Institute, 2006).

12. William Chris Hobgood, *Welcoming Resistance: A Path to Faithful Ministry* (Herndon, VA: Alban Institute, 2002).
13. Eugene H. Peterson, *Working the Angles: The Shape of Pastoral Integrity* (Grand Rapids: Eerdmans, 1987).
14. Tracy Schier, "The First Parish Project of the Hinton Rural Life Center: Where 'Small Is Beautiful,'" Resources for American Christianity, http://resourcingchristianity.org.
15. Ibid., 3.
16. Cited at www.bethanyfellowships.org.
17. For more on these and other issues facing pastors in their first congregational call, see *Congregations* 32, no. 4 (Fall 2006), published by the Alban Institute, http://www.alban.org/book-details.aspx?id=3920.

Chapter 4, Autumn in Ministry: Endurance and Transformation

1. Thomas Merton, *The Wisdom of the Desert* (San Francisco: New Directions, 1970), 50.
2. Heidi B. Neumark, *Breathing Space: A Spiritual Journey in the South Bronx* (New York: Beacon Press, 2003), 97.
3. Ibid., 98.
4. Thich Nhat Hanh, *Peace Is Every Step* (New York: Bantam Books, 1991).
5. Herbert Benson, *Timeless Healing: The Power and Biology of Belief* (New York: Scribners, 1997).
6. Barbara Brown Taylor, *Leaving Church: A Memoir of Faith* (New York: HarperOne, 2007), 75.
7. Ibid., 102.
8. Judith Viorst, *Necessary Losses: The Loves, Illusions, Dependencies, and Impossible Expectations That All of Us Have to Give Up in Order to Grow* (New York: Free Press, 1998).
9. Granger E. Westberg, *Good Grief* (Minneapolis: Fortress Press, 2004).
10. Whitehead, *Process and Reality*, 102.

11. Roy M. Oswald and Robert E. Friedrich, *Discerning Your Congregation's Future: A Strategic and Spiritual Approach* (Washington, DC: Alban Institute, 1996).

12. Walter Brueggemann, *The Prophetic Imagination* (Minneapolis: Fortress Press, 2001).

13. Neumark, *Breathing Space*, 234.

14. Bruce G. Epperly, *God's Touch: Faith, Wholeness, and the Healing Miracles of Jesus* (Louisville: Westminster/John Knox, 2001); Larry Dossey, *Healing Words: The Power of Prayer and the Practice of Medicine* (San Francisco: HarperSanFrancisco, 1994); Harold G. Koenig, *Is Religion Good for Your Health? The Effects of Religion on Physical and Mental Health* (Binghamton, NY: Haworth Press, 1997); Dale A. Matthews, *The Faith Factor: Proof of the Healing Power of Prayer* (New York: Viking, 1998).

15. Renita J. Weems, *Listening for God: A Pastor's Journey through Silence and Doubt* (New York: Simon and Schuster, 2000), 15.

16. Mother Teresa, *Mother Teresa: Come Be My Light*, ed. Brian Kolodiejchuk (New York: Doubleday, 2007).

17. Weems, *Listening for God*, 15.

18. Ibid., 21.

19. For more about Val Hastings's approach to clergy coaching, see www.coaching4clergy.com.

20. For more on the use of spiritual affirmations, see Epperly, *The Power of Affirmative Faith* and *Holy Adventure*.

Chapter 5, Winter in Ministry: Vision and Letting Go

1. Gordon M. Forbes, *Downstream* (Bethesda, MD: Authorhouse, 2007).

2. Marilynne Robinson, *Gilead* (New York: Farrar, Straus, and Giroux, 2004), 18-19.

3. For more on the challenge of integrating soul and role in ministry, see Parker Palmer, *A Hidden Wholeness: The Journey Toward an Undivided Life* (San Francisco: Jossey-Bass, 2004), 14-17.

4. Alfred North Whitehead, *Religion in the Making* (New York: Macmillan, 1926), 16.

5. Harold G. Koenig, *Aging and God: Spiritual Pathways to Mental Health in Midlife and Later Years* (Binghamton, NY: Haworth Press, 1994); Robert Raines, *A Time to Live: Seven Steps of Creative Aging* (New York: Dutton, 1998); Carroll Saussy, *The Art of Growing Old: A Guide to Faithful Aging* (Minneapolis: Augsburg Books, 2000).

6. Madeleine L'Engle, *A Ring of Endless Light* (New York: Bantam Doubleday, Dell Publishing Group, 1995), 249.

7. C. S. Lewis, *A Grief Observed* (New York: Bantam, 1976), 55.

8. M. Scott Peck, *The Road Less Traveled*, 25th anniv. ed. (New York: Simon and Schuster), 15.

9. *Book of Worship: United Church of Christ* (New York: Office of First Life and Leadership), 256.

10. Robinson, *Gilead*, 23.

11. Dag Hammarskjold, *Markings* (New York: Vintage, 2006), 89.

12. We are grateful to the insights of David Rich and Peter Schmiechen that served as the foundation of our reflections on Lancaster Theological Seminary's Harvesting Wisdom program.

13. We recommend the following texts on spiritual autobiography, writing, and vocation: Frederick Buechner, *Sacred Journey: A Memoir of Early Days* (New York: Harper Row, 1991); Buechner, *Telling Secrets* (New York: Harper Row, 1992); Julia Cameron, *The Artist's Way: A Spiritual Path to Higher Creativity* (Los Angeles: Jeremy Tarcher, 2002); Natalie Goldberg, *Writing Down the Bones: Freeing the Writer Within* (Boston: Shambala, 2006); Kent Ira Groff, *Writing Tides: Finding Grace and Growth through Writing* (Nashville: Abingdon, 2007); Palmer

J. Palmer, *Let Your Life Speak: Listening for the Voice of Vocation* (San Francisco: Jossey-Bass, 1999); and Dan Wakefield, *The Story of Your Life: Writing a Spiritual Autobiography* (Boston: Beacon Press, 1990).

14. For more on Erik Erikson's theory of the stages of personal development, see Erik Erikson, *Childhood and Society* (New York: W. W. Norton, 1993) and *Identity and the Life Cycle* (New York: W. W. Norton, 1994).